THE
COMPLETE
LETTER
WRITER

THE COMPLETE LETTER WRITER

*How to write letters
for every occasion*

foulsham
LONDON • NEW YORK • TORONTO • SYDNEY

foulsham

The Publishing House, Bennetts Close,
Cippenham, Berkshire, SL1 5AP, England

ISBN 0-572-02424-X

Printed in Great Britain by Cox & Wyman Ltd, Reading, Berkshire

CONTENTS

HOW TO USE THIS BOOK

Suppose you have a letter to write and are unsure how to approach it. It may be that you do not often write letters or, perhaps, the particular letter that is troubling you deals with something unfamiliar to you.

Whatever the problems, your first step is to run through this book and find if there is a specimen letter included which deals exactly with your subject. If there is, you can go ahead at once and follow the wording given, making whatever alterations are necessary regarding names, addresses, dates and so on.

On the other hand, if there is no specimen which fits your case exactly, there is sure to be one that deals with something similar to yours. For instance, you may want to write a letter to a person reminding them that they have not paid the rent of a garage which you lease them. There is no example referring to this matter, but there are letters referring to the overdue rent of houses. Though the things at issue are different, the way to write them is the same. So, you take one of the house letters, alter the parts that do not apply and there you have exactly what you want for garages.

In addition, by using a passage from one specimen letter and piecing it into another letter, you many be able to say more satisfactorily what you have in mind. When doing this, great care must be taken to see that the styles of the two portions agree. For instance, one part must not say 'I' and the other say 'We'.

In all cases, it is necessary to copy the arrangement and punctuation of the opening address, the date and the salutations, as any difference may make them incorrect.

It should be clear, then, that anyone who has a letter to write will find assistance in the examples that are given, no matter what the letter is about.

· 1 ·

HOW TO WRITE
A LETTER

It has been said that 'the letter you write is you'. If this is so, it is very certain that every letter we send out should be our best work, in order that the recipient may get a good impression of us.

A good letter calls for many qualities. The content should be well phrased and written, or typed, the paper should be of suitable quality, the envelope properly addressed and spaced, the stamp stuck on in the right place and so on.

Let's consider these things in detail. First, the notepaper. This should be of good quality, plain with nothing fancy such as deckled edges or coloured borders. Sheets of A4 size are best for all but personal correspondence. The paper and the envelope should match except when several sheets are enclosed in a large envelope.

Start by writing your own address in full, then give the date. Both these should be placed close to the upper right-hand corner.

On a level with the date, but on the left of the paper, write the name and address of the person who is to receive the letter, if it is a business communication, and, on the next line, follow with the opening 'Dear Sir', 'Dear Madam', 'Sir', 'Madam', or whatever is appropriate. If, however, it is a friendly letter, start with 'Dear Joan', 'Dear Miss Smith', 'Dear Fred', or whatever is correct in the circumstances.

Then, having set out the preliminaries, start with the actual letter. The opening sentence will probably be the hardest to compose, because once you have managed to make a beginning, the subsequent passages will follow naturally. If you cannot think of a suitable beginning, look at the list on page 13 or glance through the specimen letters in this book; there ought to be dozens that will suit your purpose.

But, whatever you do, do not be tempted to start off with that ghastly cliché, 'I trust you are well, as this leaves me at present'.

It is much better to say nothing about your own health until reaching the end of the letter, and then only in a friendly letter. A good way to mention it is to say something like this: 'All of us at home are very well and we hope that you are too'.

Business letters often begin with the formula, 'I acknowledge receipt of your letter of so and so and in reply ...'. This is straightforward and to the point, and it also links up in the mind of the recipient some former communication.

Having plunged into the letter, get to the real facts at once. Say what you have to say clearly and briefly and do not use involved sentences which may have two or more meanings. Use straightforward language and only ever words you fully understand.

Do not be tempted to use the third person in expressing yourself, unless you are dealing with a formal invitation and, of course, you must not mix up the first and third person in the same letter. Some years ago, I came across a letter in which this mixing of persons was beautifully illustrated. The letter began 'Dear Sir, Mrs Brown presents her compliments and I would like to know why the goods I ordered have not yet arrived'.

After brevity, the next consideration is courtesy. There's no need to be either haughty or servile. If you have anything unpleasant to say, think twice or even three times before you say it. Personally, I have written many letters with a sting in them, but I never post such letters for at least 24 hours to give myself a safety valve. Often I then rewrite the letter or throw it in the bin.

Frame your remarks in a composed style, not in the

breathless haste which suggests a whirlwind. We all know the kind of person who tells us that they are in a 'terrific hurry' or are 'dreadfully busy'. What we are really being told is that they begrudge the time that is being wasted on writing to us. And next to the whirlwind type of letter is the gushing letter in which things are 'absolutely beautiful' and everybody is a darling. Such remarks are tiresome.

Never commit yourself to libellous statements in a letter or scandalous gossip. It is unnecessary and risky.

Certain hackneyed phrases are best avoided. People write, 'Referring to your letter and thanking you for same'. The word 'same', used in this way, stamps the writer as a person with a poor mastery of words. 'Re:' at the head of a letter can help to save time in tracing matters, but 're' in the body of a letter is usually poor, e.g., 'I saw Mr Jones, yesterday re what we were discussing'. Latin abbreviations such as 'ult.', 'inst.' and 'prox.' should be used sparingly. Far better give the actual name of the month.

Always put the date on your letter; make sure that the recipient's name and initials are given correctly; read the letter over before sealing it; check the facts and figures, if any, and be sure, if enclosures are mentioned, that they really are enclosed. Finally, make certain that you put the letter in the right envelope.

Business letters

Letters sent out from a business address should be printed on one side only of good-quality paper. If the paper has no printed letter heading, the address of the sender should appear at the top in full. A little lower down on the left-hand side of the paper, the name of the recipient should appear. The salutation – 'Dear Sir', 'Dear Madam', 'Sir' or 'Madam' – as the case may be should follow, and under this a heading, underlined if possible, as 'Re: Your Outstanding Account'. The subject matter follows. This should be concise, but not laconic. Decide what you want to say and say it in the fewest possible words consistent with politeness. The sentences should not be too long and the whole thing should be broken up into reasonably short paragraphs.

When single-space typing is used for the body of the letter, leave one line space between the paragraphs. If the letter is short, double spacing looks better, but use single spacing for a long one. Block style (i.e. without indentation at the beginning of paragraphs) is most commonly used nowadays. However, if you prefer an indented style, about five spaces may be left on the left-hand side of the paper when starting a fresh paragraph. All letters look better if a fairly wide margin is left.

Do not be florid or servile. Do not drop into the lazy habit of using stereotyped jargon. Pay your clients the compliment of writing a different letter to each, even though writing about the same subject matter to all. Conclude a business letter with 'Yours faithfully'.

If there is any enclosure, it is a good plan to write 'Enclosure' or 'Encs.' in the bottom left-hand corner of the sheet. Always sign a letter by hand – it does not take long to sign your name. If your signature in illegible, it is a good plan to print your name (in brackets) under the signature.

Fold the letter neatly and evenly two or three times, according to the size of the envelope. The cover should be addressed exactly in accordance with the heading of the letter. If a window envelope is used, fold the letter with the writing outside, and place in the envelope with the address showing through the transparency. See that all enclosures are in the envelope before sealing up. Finally, make sure you put on the correct amount of stamps; an amazingly large number of packages are placed in the letter boxes without any stamps at all!

How to begin a letter

(1) Dear Sir
(2) Dear Madam
Either of the above is usual in all business correspondence.

(3) Sir
(4) Madam
These are equally appropriate, but rather more severe.
(5) Dear Sirs
This is the correct opening when the letter is addressed to 'Messrs So and So'. As an alternative 'Sirs' can be used.
(6) Dear Mr Jones
(7) Dear Mrs Brown
(8) Dear Miss Smith
All the above are correct when a less formal approach is required.
(9) Dear Miss
This is never correct and should never be written.
(10) Dear Tom or My Dear Tom
(11) Dear Alice or My Dear Alice
To be used when the friendship between writer and receiver is close.
(12) My Darling Tom, My Dearest Mary
These are correct for special cases of affection.

Phrases for beginning letters

If you are hesitating for a phrase with which to open your letter, probably one of the following will suit your purpose:

In reply to your letter of
It was very good of you to
I am sorry to have to say that
It is so long since you wrote that
I wonder if you could
In accordance with your request
Please accept my thanks for
Enclosed please find
Would you be good enough to
Many thanks for your letter of
I regret to inform you that
I must thank you for

I greatly appreciate your
I acknowledge your letter of
I refer to your letter of
Thank you for
I am anxious to hear from you about
You may be interested to hear
We wish to remind you that
I have to tell you that
Your letter gave me
I have carefully considered your
Recently, we had occasion to write to you about
I am pleased to confirm your letter of
With reference to your letter of
It is with considerable pleasure (regret) that I
Many thanks for the beautiful
You will be sorry, I know, to hear that
I find it necessary to

How to close a letter

(1) Yours faithfully

A safe ending for all business letters starting 'Dear Sir' or 'Dear Madam'.

(2) Yours truly and Yours very truly

Correct for business letters, when something a little more friendly than (1) is required, but not much used nowadays.

(3) Yours sincerely

A safe ending for all personal letters and business letters starting 'Dear Mr Jones', 'Dear Mrs Smith', etc.

(4) Yours affectionately

Suitable for relations, would-be relations and between girl friends, but now usually replaced by (3).

(5) Yours cordially

Used by rather old-fashioned people who wish to write something not so ordinary as (3).

(6) Yours respectfully

Not advised as it is too servile.

(7) Yours

Only to be used when writing to a close friend.

The address on the notepaper

(1) Do not give the name of a house in inverted commas. Thus, write Pembridge, not 'Pembridge'.

(2) It is correct to follow the number of the house by a comma, but nowadays most people omit it.

(3) At the end of all lines in the address, a comma may be used, except in the case of the last line, when a full stop is required. However, it is now acceptable to omit punctuation altogether in addresses.

The date

Every letter should be dated.

The date may come after the address of the sender, on the right-hand side of the sheet, or above the address of the recipient, on the left.

There are many ways in which it can be given correctly. For example:

(1) January 1, 19—

(2) Jan. 3, 19—

(3) 4 January, 19—

(4) January 2nd, 19—

(5) 5 Jan., 19—

(6) Jan. 6th, 19—

(7) 7 : 1 : 97

(8) 8/1/97

Forms (7) and (8) should be generally avoided.

Note that in America, forms (7) and (8) are reordered so that the month precedes the day.

It is common nowadays to drop the full stop after abbreviations such as Jan.

Addressing an envelope

The address on an envelope gives the recipient their first impression of what is likely to be inside. If it is well written, the impression will be a good one, but if the wording is badly arranged, it will certainly be less favourable.

To space the wording properly, imagine a horizontal line cutting the envelope into two. Start writing the name slightly below the imaginary line. If your handwriting is large and the address is rather long, begin on the imaginary line, or even a little higher. Start writing slightly in from the left-hand edge.

Below the name set out the address in two, three or more lines, as necessary. Each line can be indented a little more than the one above, or, if you prefer a block style, begin each fresh line absolutely flush with the line above, as in examples Nos. 5–8 below.

Fix the stamp in the upper right-hand corner; it should be put on straight. To tilt it or place it upside down is considered by some to be a breach of etiquette.

Here are some specimens worth noting:

(1) B.A.Williams Esq.
    Hatcherley
     Lane End
      Brighton
       BN3 5UD

(2) Mr Bertram Davidson
    38, Victoria Road
     Westbridge
     Surrey
      KT13 5NE

(3) James Phillips Esq., M.P.
    House of Commons
     London
      SW1 4PQ

(4) Mrs Bertram Davidson
    38, Victoria Road
     Westbridge
     Surrey
      KT13 5NE

(5) Miss Alice Turnbull
    51 Cadogan Row
    Wigan
    Lancs
    W13 4GR

(6) Messrs Warren & Bourne
    Timber Merchants
    3 Green Road
    West Bridgford
    Nottinghamshire
    N16 2OU

(7) The Thames Timber Co. Ltd
    54 Wharf Lane
    London
    EC1 9XP

(8) <u>Please forward</u>
    Mrs M. Eagles
    16 Derrymore Street
    Pimlico
    London
    SW1 4BU

Let us look at these eight examples:

(1) uses 'Esq.', and (2) uses 'Mr'. These are alternative modes of address. You can use one or the other, but never both since they mean exactly the same. To write 'Mr B.A. Williams Esq.' would be a bad mistake. It is also wrong to write out 'Esquire' in full.

(3) shows that abbreviated titles come after the designation 'Esq.'. Thus 'James Phillips, M.P., Esq.' is wrong.

Although we are using full punctuation here, with full stops after all the abbreviated words, many people no longer bother with this. It would be considered perfectly correct, therefore, to write 'Mr BA Williams Esq' with no full stops at all. Note that a full stop is never required after 'Mr' as the abbreviation ends with the same letter as the full word. The same rule applies to Dr, Revd (do not use Rev.), Mrs, Messrs and Ms.

(4) shows that in addressing a married woman, it is traditional to give her husband's Christian name. It used to be considered wrong to write 'Mrs Mary Davidson', unless she was widowed or divorced, however, this is now becoming acceptable and in fact many women prefer this form and find the traditional use offensive.

(5) there is no full stop after 'Miss' because it is not an abbreviated word.

(6) and (7) show that 'Messrs' should only be employed in the form of address to a firm whose name incorporates individual surnames.

(8) is a request that the letter should be redirected to an address not known by the writer.

The Post Office requests writers to adhere to the following rules, to save time and so speed up delivery:

(1) Use the number of the house, if it has one, and not just the name of the house.

(2) In the case of flats, chambers and suites of offices, the number of the flat etc. and its floor or block should be included.

(3) The area postcode must always be included.

(4) In country districts, the nearest post town should be given in addition to the actual village, hamlet, etc.

(5) Do not use the name of the county town, when the name of the county is intended. Thus do not write 'Cambridge' when 'Cambridgeshire' is correct.

(6) Do not write 'Local'; use the name of the post town.

Using postcards

Postcards provide a handy, quick and cheap way of sending messages. They are best used to send a hurried note, but it should be quite impersonal. There should be nothing of a private or intimate nature in what is written. After all the writer may be somewhat thick-skinned and not mind how much of their affairs is made public, but they should think of the receiver who probably does mind.

Remember, if you expose private business on a postcard, your friends may not thank you.

Writing to persons of title

When writing to titled people, it is important to use the form of address appropriate to their rank: The list of titles below gives the correct way to (1) address the envelope, (2) start the letter and (3) close the letter.

The Queen: (1) Her Most Gracious Majesty Queen Elizabeth II. (2) Madam, OR May it please your Majesty. (3) I have the honour to remain, your Majesty's most faithful servant.

Royal Princes: (1) His Royal Highness (then give title) (2) Sir. (3) I have the honour to remain, Sir, Your Royal Highness's most dutiful servant.

Royal Princesses: (1) Her Royal Highness (then give title) (2) Madam. (3) I have the honour to remain, Madam, your Royal Highness's most dutiful servant.

Other Princes and Princesses: As for royal princesses, but omit 'Royal' and 'most'.

Duke: (1) His Grace the Duke of —. (2) My Lord Duke. (3) I remain, my Lord Duke, your Grace's most obedient servant.

Duchess: (1) Her Grace the Duchess of —. (2) Madam. (3) I remain, Madam, your Grace's most obedient servant.

Marquess: (1) The Most Honourable, the Marquess of —. (2) My Lord Marquess. (3) I remain, my Lord Marquess, your

Lordship's most obedient servant.

Marchioness: (1) The Most Honourable, The Marchioness of —. (2) Madam. (3) I remain, Madam, your Ladyship's most obedient servant.

Earl: (1) The Right Honourable the Earl of —. (2) My Lord. (3) I remain, my Lord, your Lordship's most obedient servant.

Countess: (1) The Right Honourable the Countess of —. (2) and (3) As for a Marchioness.

Viscount: (1) The Right Honourable the Lord Viscount —. (2) and (3) As for an Earl.

Viscountess: (1) The Right Honourable the Lady Viscountess —. (2) and (3) As for a Marchioness.

Baron: (1) The Right Honourable Lord —. (2) and (3) As for an Earl.

Baroness: (1) The Right Honourable Lady —. (2) and (3) As for a Marchioness.

Baronet: (1) Sir (Christian and surname), Bt. (not Bart.) (2) Sir. (3) No special form.

Baronet's wife: (1) Lady (surname only, unless born with a title.) (2) Madam. (3) No special form

Archbishop: (1) His Grace the Lord Archbishop of —. (2) My Lord Archbishop. (3) I remain, my Lord Archbishop, your Grace's most obedient servant.

Bishop: (1) The Right Reverend the Lord Bishop of —. (2) My Lord Bishop, Very Reverend Sir. (3) I remain, My Lord Bishop, your Lordship's most obedient servant.

Dean (1) The Very Reverend the Dean of —. (2) Very Reverend Sir. (3) I remain, Reverend Sir, your most obedient servant.

Archdeacon: (1) The Venerable the Archdeacon —. (2) Reverend Sir. (3) As for a Dean.

Ambassador: (1) His Excellency HBM's Ambassador and Plenipotentiary to the Court of —. (2) and (3) According to rank. HBM stands for Her Britannic Majesty.

Ambassador's wife: According to rank.

Governor General: (1) His Excellency —, Governor

General of —; OR, if a Duke, His Grace the Governor General of —. (2) and (3) According to rank.

Governor of Colony: (1) His Excellency —, Governor of —. (2) and (3) According to rank.

British Consul: (1) —. Esq., HBM's Agent and Consul (OR Vice Consul, OR Consul General, as case may be) No special formula for (2) or (3)

Prime Minister: According to rank.

Privy Councillor: (1) To the Right Hon. —. (2) and (3) According to rank.

Secretary of State: (1) Her Majesty's Principal Secretary of State for the — Department. (2) and (3) According to rank.

Lord Mayor: (1) To the Right Hon. the Lord Mayor of —. (2) My Lord. (3) Your Lordship's obedient servant.

Mayor (of a city OR of Hastings, Rye, Hythe, New Romney): (1) The Right Worshipful the Mayor of —; (of a town) The Worshipful the Mayor of —. (2) Sir. (3) I remain, Sir, your obedient servant.

Judge (England and Northern Ireland): (1) The Hon. Sir — (if a Knight) OR The Hon. Mr Justice —. (2) Sir. (3) I have the honour to be, Sir, your most obedient servant.

County Court Judge: (1) To His Honour, Judge —. (2) and (3) As above.

Scottish Judge (Lord of Session): (1) The Hon. Lord —. (2) My Lord. (3) I have the honour to be, your Lordship's most obedient servant.

Writing to a person with Honours and M.P.s

Knight: (1) Sir —. (2) Sir. (3) No special form.

Knight's wife: As for Baronet's wife.

CBE, OBE, MBE: As in private life, with the addition of their letters after their name. If using esquire, place their letters after Esq.

Member of Parliament: As in private life, with the addition of the letters M.P. after the name. If using esquire, place M.P. after Esq.

· 2 ·

INVITATIONS
AND REPLIES

All sorts of invitations are dealt with in this section. The necessary replies – acceptances or refusals – are also given.

Formal invitation to dinner

Ridgway House
Ridgway Lane
Reigate
RE9 4DP
22 January 19—

My dear Susan

Would you like to come over, with John, for dinner here on Thursday, February 10th? It would be just right if you arrived about 6.30 p.m.

There will be a few friends here, but you have met them all before.

After dinner, if there is time, we hope to get in a few hands of bridge.

Do write back and say that John and you can both manage it. We have not seen you for ages.

With love
Marjorie

Letter accepting a formal invitation to dinner

Northcote
Charlwood Drive
Reigate
RE4 3XL
29 January 19—

My dear Marjorie

How nice of you to ask us both to come to dinner on February 10th.

John and I are delighted to accept your invitation and we are looking forward to a very enjoyable evening.

John sends his love.

With love
Susan

Note that the letter repeats the date, so that if, by any chance, a mistake has been made, the fact will be brought to light and corrected.

Invitation to dinner (semi-formal)

Ridgway House
Ridgway Lane
Reigate
RE9 4DP
22 January 19—

Dear Mrs Bolton

Would you and your husband like to join us for dinner on Thursday February 10th at 6.30 p.m.?

We are asking a few friends, all of whom you have met here before. Afterwards, we hope to have some time for bridge.

It will be very nice if you can come and we very much hope that you will.

Yours sincerely
Marjorie Summers

Letter accepting an invitation

Northcote
Charlwood Drive
Reigate
RE4 3XL
29 January 19—

Dear Mrs Summers

Very many thanks for your kind invitation. My husband and I will be delighted to come to dinner on February 10th.

I need hardly tell you that we are both looking forward to seeing you.

Yours sincerely
Patricia Bolton

Note that a wife can speak or write of her husband in three ways. She can use his first name; she can refer to him as 'my husband'; or she can speak of him as 'Mr So-and-so'. If he is well known to the person receiving the letter, then the first name is suitable. 'My husband' is safe in any circumstances. The form 'Mr So-and-so' is now used only in conversation with employees and should therefore not be used in social correspondence.

Letter refusing an invitation (semi-formal)

Northcote
Charlwood Drive
Reigate
RE4 3XL
29 January 19—

Dear Mrs Summers

Very many thanks for your kind invitation to dinner on February 10th. Unfortunately, my husband will be out of the country on business on that date, so we shall not be able to be with you. We are both very sorry. Very many thanks.

Yours sincerely
Patricia Bolton

Formal invitation to a wedding
(to be printed)

Dr and Mrs Mervyn Giles
request the pleasure of
the company of
★ Miss Lucy Thompson ★
at the marriage of their daughter, Susan,
to
Mr Graham Jones,
at Holy Trinity Church, Mexford,
on Saturday, April 3rd, 19—, at 2 o'clock
and afterwards at
Gunter's Hall, Mexford.

RSVP
The Hall, Mexford, MX10 3DG.

On a printed invitation, the name of the guest (starred) will be added by hand. The reply should be in the third person, as below.

Reply to a formal wedding invitation

The Red Roofs
Mexford
MX2 9BD

20 February 19—

Miss Lucy Thompson thanks Dr and Mrs Mervyn Giles for their kind invitation to be present at the wedding of their daughter, Susan, to Mr Graham Jones, which she has much pleasure in accepting.

OR

Miss Lucy Thompson has much pleasure in accepting the kind invitation of Dr and Mrs Mervyn Giles to be present at the wedding of their daughter, Susan, to Mr Graham Jones.

Formal invitation to a dance
(to be printed)

Mr and Mrs A.E. Clarke
request the pleasure of the company of
★ Mr and Mrs James Stoneham ★
on Saturday, December 4th, 19—.

The Horns
Chertsey Vale　　　　　　　　Dancing 9.30 p.m. – 2.30 a.m.
ST9 8EU　　　　　　　　　　　　　　　　　　　RSVP

OR

Mrs A.E. Clarke
requests the pleasure of the company of
★ Miss Jennifer Waters ★
on Thursday, January 8th, 19—.

The Horns
Chertsey Vale　　　　　　　　Dancing 8.30 p.m. – 1 a.m.
ST9 8EU　　　　　　　　　　　　　　　　　　　RSVP

Reply to a formal invitation

The Hollyhocks
Chertsey Vale
ST9 8TP
26 November 19—
Mr and Mrs James Stoneham wish to thank Mr and Mrs
A.E. Clarke for their kind invitation for December 4th and
have much pleasure in accepting.

OR

… and much regret that a prior engagement prevents them
from accepting.

'At home' invitation
(to be printed)

Mrs B. Harris
Mr and Mrs Arthur Prince
At Home
4 – 6.30 p.m. Thursday, December 18th.

Ferndale
Snake's Lane
Burton
BN27 9AE

An 'at home' invitation is sent out on an engraved printed card, the wording being as above. The name of the person invited (starred) is handwritten on the card. Thus, in this case, Mrs Harris is invited by Mr and Mrs Prince. No acceptance or refusal is needed. Friends merely 'drop in'.

Invitation to a twenty-first birthday party
(to be printed)

61 Tregunter Park
Fulham
SW6 9TK
10 March 19—

Captain and Mrs David Brown
request the pleasure of
Miss Alice Mackenzie
at an evening party
to be held on April 2nd, at 8.45 p.m.
at the above address to
celebrate the coming of age
of their daughter
Vivienne

RSVP

Invitation to a children's party

17 Burnside Avenue
South Ham
Essex
HA5 2JB
12 December 19—

Dear Mrs Alston

Marion and David are having a few of their friends to a party here, on Tuesday, January 3rd from 4.30 to 9 p.m., and they are hoping that John will be able to come.

If you are thinking of coming to fetch him, it would be nice if you arrived about 7 p.m. Then, you would be in time to see some of the fun.

Do try to come, as I shall be so pleased to see you.

Yours sincerely
Mary Seymour

This letter is, of course, written by the mother of Marion and David.

Letter accepting an invitation to a children's party

24 Burnside Avenue
South Ham
Essex
HA5 2JB
22 December 19—

Dear Mrs Seymour

Thank you very much for inviting John to Marion and David's party. He is excited about it and is looking forward to coming.

I will drop in about 7 p.m., as you suggest, just to have a chat.

Looking forward to seeing you,

Yours sincerely
Marjorie Alston

Letter refusing an invitation to a children's party

24 Burnside Avenue
South Ham
Essex
HA5 2JB
22 December 19—

Dear Mrs Seymour

John is most upset, but he will not be able to accept the invitation for the party on January 3rd.

We always spend Christmas with my husband's family down in Devon and we shall be away a fortnight.

Please thank Marion and David and tell them how sorry John is that he will not be able to come.

It was very nice of you to ask him.

Yours sincerely
Marjorie Alston

Letter inviting a friend on a driving holiday

The Grey Towers
Littlebourne
Kent
LB10 9DX
1 July 19—

Dear Helen

Will you come and join us on a little driving holiday? George is terribly proud of the new car he has just bought and we plan to have a lovely tour through Wales. If you can come – and we are really keen that you should join us – there will be you, George, myself and my brother Bill. I think you have met Bill – anyway, he is quite sure he remembers you – so we ought to make a nice little party. We thought of starting from here about the beginning of next month. George will be mapping out the tour beforehand; of course it can be changed if anybody has any suggestions to make – but he will find out in advance where are the best hotels and stopping-places. Will

you say which day you can come? A few days before we start
would be best, so that we can settle things and get off
comfortably.

Yours with love

Christine

Reply to an invitation to take part in a driving holiday

Middle Cloisters

Canterbury

CA4 5DP

7 July 19—

Dear Christine

How good of you to ask me to join you! I should love to
come! Let's hope the weather will be good. Tell me what
clothes I shall want, and about how long you propose to be
on tour.

I have always wanted to see Caernarvon and Betws-y-
Coed; but there are so many lovely places in Wales that I shall
be quite happy to fit in with your plans. Perhaps we could go
to Tintern and Chepstow and Raglan. If I come to you on the
28th, will that suit you?

Yours, filled with anticipation,

Helen

Letter inviting a friend to stay

Cranford

Middle Haven

Devon

MH19 4XP

3 August 19—

My dear Sheila

You have heard, I believe, from Mother that we are all
down here, enjoying ourselves immensely. The weather so far

has been perfect and the sea air is really doing us good. Everything seems to be combining to make our holiday a great success.

But my point in writing is to ask if you will come and join us? Indeed, I will not ask, I'll just say – you <u>must</u> come and join us.

Come and stay a fortnight as soon as you can. I feel sure you will have an enjoyable time and will be all the better for the fresh air.

Don't bother to bring a whole wardrobe full of dresses: everything is very casual. As you know, Father is keen on golf, so perhaps you would like to bring your clubs.

Drop me a note saying when you will come. I need hardly add that Jim will be extremely put out if you don't!

Yours sincerely
Janet

Letter accepting an invitation to stay with friends

5 Trelawny Terrace
SW20 4EE
10 August 19—

Dear Janet

I cannot tell you how delighted I was to receive your letter. It is more than kind of you to think of me, at a time when you are all enjoying yourselves so much.

I just need a lazy holiday by the sea and you seem to have planned one for me that fits in exactly with what I would like.

It will be lovely to spend some time with your family and I am looking forward to meeting Jim again.

I can arrive next Thursday, 16th August, reaching Middle Haven at 5.15 p.m. Is this convenient for you?

Yours sincerely
Sheila

Letter of invitation for a Christmas visit

The Doves
Eckford
Kent
EK10 4XZ
10 December 19—

My dearest Sallie

We would like you to come and help us to enjoy Christmas this year. Could you come on the 23rd and stay for a week? The boys come home that day and if you can join their train, or arrive about the same time, James can meet you all and bring your luggage together. But if that does not quite fit in with your plans, never mind. Something else can be arranged.

We are having a children's party, a dance for the grown-ups and several other events during the week: so please don't think of refusing.

With love from us all,

Yours sincerely
Kate Pershore

Letter of invitation to a christening

38 Pope's Drive
Bankford
Durham
D23 4NH
2 April 19—

Dear Mary

Sunday, April 17th, is a red-letter day for David. He is to be christened at St Paul's Church, Bankford, at 2.30 p.m.

You have always shown such interest in our son and heir and so Will and I would be delighted if you would join us at the ceremony.

We should like you to arrive around 1.30 p.m. and stay the rest of the day.

Will sends his kind regards.

Yours sincerely
Patricia

Letter refusing the invitation to a christening

40 Byron's Avenue
Bankford
Durham
D23 6NB
9 April 19—

Dear Patricia

I hope you will forgive me when I tell you that I am unable to come to David's christening.

My mother is far from well and I do not think I ought to leave her. She has been ailing now for some weeks and misses me when I am not with her.

It was kind of you to ask me and I am sure you know that, in happier circumstances, I should have been delighted to come.

My love to Will and the baby.

Yours sincerely
Mary

· 3 ·

LOVE AND
MARRIAGE

Love letters in general

Love letters are the most highly personal of all forms of
correspondence and it would be misleading to try to lay
down any rules for this sort of writing. There is only
one worthwhile rule and that is simply: 'Be yourself'. Write
naturally and without any affectation. Do not try for any
highly literary style, or your letters will sound artificial. The
best thing is to write as you talk to your loved one.

A word of warning, however: beware of making a definite
promise in writing that you may not want to keep. Love is a
matter of emotions, but marriage concerns reason as well; do
not allow yourself to be carried away by your feelings at the
expense of your common sense.

The normal rules for beginning and ending letters do not
apply to love letters. All couples have their own pet ways, and
in fact originality is half the charm of a love letter. 'My dearest
Joe', 'My darling Becky', or simply 'Darling' are all good
openings in the appropriate circumstances. The word 'love'
cannot very well be left out of the ending, although the exact
wording of this is entirely a matter of taste.

Do not overdo the endearments or they will begin to lose
their value. Send kisses by all means but do not decorate half
a page with x's, as this looks rather cheap and silly. Above all,
do not put x's or cryptic letters on the backs of envelopes. A
person receiving letters in envelopes decorated in this way
may be subjected to a great deal of teasing from his or her

family and it may have the opposite effect from that intended.

Here is quite an ordinary letter from a man to his girlfriend. They have already declared their love for each other, and although they are not formally engaged they have a definite though private understanding between themselves. The letter is just an example of one style of writing a love letter.

———

Love letter from a man

3 Chiswick Terrace
Bristol
BS8 5TK
18 March 19—

Darling

Monday again – and another dreary Monday, because I've got to wait five long days before I see you again. I should be feeling utterly miserable if I hadn't got so many wonderful hopes and memories to keep me company. And after all, it was only yesterday that we were together, so I really ought not to grumble.

Jenny dearest, I tried to tell you last night how much I love you and I don't think I said half of what I really meant. I thought I might make up for that in this letter – and now I'm even more stuck for words. I'll have another go next weekend!

As you will guess, I'm writing this in my lunch-hour and old Tom Smith is peering over his specs, hoping to see what I'm doing, but trying hard not to let me know it. I wonder if he ever wrote letters like this to Mrs S? It's hard to believe!

It's just on two now, so I must pack up and get back to the grindstone. Goodbye, sweetheart. I'll write again before Saturday. And I'll think of you all the time.

Your own loving
Daniel

Reply to a love letter from a man

340 Longland Road
Cheltenham
CE10 5BZ
22 March 19—

My dearest Daniel

Mummy is giving me some real old-fashioned looks over the breakfast table these days, and the postman is getting downright nosey. Daddy goes on reading the paper and pretends not to notice.

I hate to think of you sitting at your desk with only Tom Smith to keep you company. But it's the same for me, you know. My days at work aren't any more delightful than yours and Bob Taylor is just as much a silly old bore as your Tom Smith. But he did mention what a nice bracelet I was wearing this morning. 'Is it a new one?' he asked casually and he was dying to know who had given it to me.

Darling, I'm just as fed up waiting for weekends as you are, but I feel a lot better when I get your letters. I've got quite a bundle now and they've all been read lots of times.

You know I'm not very good at expressing my feelings, especially in letters – but you do know that I love you, don't you, Daniel? Because I do – more than I can say.

Your own
Jenny

Proposals of marriage in general

Proposals of marriage are almost invariably made verbally and this method is always preferable to writing. The reasons are obvious! Shyness is a poor excuse and even a stammered proposal is more likely to be favourably received than a beautifully written letter. Anyone who writes instead of speaks because he fears a refusal is more likely to be refused this way.

Therefore, a proposal should be made by letter only when

there are special circumstances that make a verbal proposal impossible. The most usual circumstance is a long distance between the two parties. If it is impossible to overcome this – as it may be, for example, when the separation is due to service in the forces, or overseas employment – then a letter is justified.

Courtship by correspondence, like the more normal form of courtship, should be done gradually and the man should have led up to the proposal in previous letters. The woman should try to give him an idea of her feelings in her replies, so that he will not make a definite proposal unless he has reason to believe that it will be favourably received.

The form of the letter containing the proposal will naturally depend to a great extent on the previous correspondence. The important thing is that there should not be any noticeable change of style and therefore the following example should be modified with this in mind.

Letter proposing marriage

PO Box No 525
Bombay
India
4 June 19—

My dearest Emma

I don't know how many times I have complained in my letters about our continued separation and I think that you have guessed by now that there is a pretty deep reason behind this complaint. This separation is even worse at the moment than it has ever been because, dearest, I do not feel able to put off any longer asking you a question that I had been hoping to voice in different circumstances. I think you know what is coming, so here goes: darling, will you marry me?

You know that I love you and since we parted two months ago my feelings have grown even stronger. I couldn't ask you then, because we hadn't known each other long and in any case I expected to be home again soon. I meant to wait until I got back – but I just can't.

I know that I can't offer you much – not even myself just now – and goodness knows how much longer I shall be stuck out here. But there must be an end to it soon, and the waiting will be less dreary if I can think that the end will be the beginning of a new life with you as my wife.

I don't suppose I should have put it quite this way if you had been with me, but it isn't easy to express feelings of this sort in a letter. I only hope you can read between the lines and guess just how much I really love and want you.

Yours, for ever if you want me, darling,
Richard

Reply to a proposal of marriage

49 Oakfields Road
Bath
BA12 8NQ
19 June 19—

My dearest Richard

Oh, yes, yes, YES!

Is it rather unladylike to snap up your proposal like that, before you had the chance to change your mind? Well, too bad. I suppose I ought to have said, 'This is so sudden', but the fact is that it was nothing of the kind. You gave me a pretty broad hint in your last letter – and when I replied I tried to give you the green light. In fact, I made up my mind weeks ago.

Richard, I know we can't fix a date and I'm as fed up about this separation as you are. It's no good asking you to be patient, because I'm so terribly impatient myself. We must just hope and dream.

Mummy and Daddy are writing to you separately – but I can tell you now they are very pleased. I can't tell you how I feel – at the moment I'm just over the moon with excitement and can't even eat. I think of you all the time and dream about our future together. To say I'm on cloud nine just doesn't come near it! Darling Richard, I love you so much.

I'll write again when I've calmed down a bit. Until then, dearest,

Yours for ever
Emma

Letter turning down a proposal of marriage

49 Oakfields Road
Bath
BA12 8NQ
19 June 19—

My dear Richard

You have paid me the greatest compliment any girl can receive and the least I can do is to give you a direct answer. And, Richard, I am afraid the answer is no.

Reading your letter made me feel very guilty. It never occurred to me that you were leading up to this in your previous letters and if I seemed to give you encouragement I assure you it was not intended. If we had been seeing each other instead of just writing I'm sure this would never have happened.

I owe you a reason at least for refusing. It would be easy for me to say that we hadn't know each other long enough or that I'm not really sure about my feelings towards you. But that would be unfair. It might make you go on wasting your hopes on me; and they really would be wasted.

Richard, please don't take it too much to heart when I say I don't want to marry you. I like you tremendously – more than any other man I know. But I'm not in love with you; and – please don't be hurt – I never shall be.

Richard, I like and admire you and you mustn't feel bad. I've risked hurting your feelings because I don't want you to waste your time hoping that I'll change when I know I shan't.

And I know you'll move on in your life and find someone much better for you than I am.

I hope you will always think of me as

Your very sincere friend

Emma

———

Letter postponing an answer to a proposal of marriage

49 Oakfields Road
Bath
BA12 8NQ
19 June 19—

My dear Richard

I have just received your letter asking me to marry you, and now I should write back yes or no. Richard, I can't. I like you very much – you know that; but I honestly don't know whether I love you. I didn't know you long enough while you were still in England and I shan't really know how I feel until I see you again.

The other side of the picture is that you may find that I'm not quite all you imagine now that you can't see me and I should hate you to come back and find that you didn't love your fiancée after all.

If I seemed to encourage you to make a proposal, I'm sorry. I didn't mean to.

I know that this 'she didn't say yes, didn't say no' line is unsatisfactory and I know that I may regret it. But I can't see any alternative.

May I make a suggestion? Let's go on writing to each other as before and see how it works out. But no ties yet. If either of us meets someone else, the other has no claim. There's one more thing, Richard. I haven't met anyone else yet. But if I do I'll tell you at once. I expect you to do the same – for both our sakes.

Yours ever

Emma

A letter like the above should only be written if the writer sincerely means every word of it. In the interests of herself as well as of her lover a woman should never postpone a definite answer to a proposal if she can possibly help it.

Letter announcing an engagement

> 52 Cherry Gardens
> Portsmouth
> PO2 3BL
> 17 April 19—

Dear Auntie

I am writing to tell you the most wonderful news – David and I have decided to get married!

We are not planning a long engagement, so the wedding will be in the next few months. We shall send you an invitation as soon as we have the date and the place sorted out.

I do hope you will be able to come.

> Love
> Alison

Letter congratulating a girl on her engagement

> 53 Locksley Mansions
> SW21 9LY
> 31 March 19—

Dear Anne

I have been hearing all sorts of rumours linking your name with a certain military gentleman. And today I have been told outright that you and he are engaged. Let me be one of the first to offer you my congratulations. Needless to say, he is a very lucky man and he should be congratulated too.

You will make a wonderful wife when the time comes and I look forward to visiting you in your new home.

I hope you will both be very happy.

> Yours sincerely
> Brenda

Letter congratulating a mother on the engagement of her daughter

364 Sloan Drive
SW1 9UT
15 May 19—

Dear Mrs Durrant

I was delighted to read in today's *Daily Telegraph* of the engagement of your daughter Joan to Harry Egremont.

I am writing to congratulate both you and Joan and I trust she will be very happy. It is certainly something to make you feel proud.

My husband joins with me in sending our kind regards both to you and to your husband.

Yours very sincerely
Mary Barker

Letter from a man to his fiancée after a disagreement

78 Marchmont Drive
Gloucester Road
SW3 4PB
8 September 19—

My dearest Beth

We've always agreed to be honest with each other and I'm not going to pretend to be full of abject apologies because I don't feel it. You were angry with me and, as I said at the time, I thought you were unfair. I still think so – but I realise that I did not help matters by the way I reacted.

I don't mind admitting that I've felt pretty fed up since our row. I want to make it up – but I know you wouldn't think much of me if I tried to get round you by taking all the blame. I reckon it's about fifty-fifty and I hope you'll agree to forget the whole thing.

Darling, I love you as much as I ever did. When can I come round and kiss and make up?

Your loving
Jonathan

Letter from a girl after a disagreement

49 Doncaster Street
N20 9KU
10 September 19—

My dearest Jonathan

You've made me feel absolutely awful. I've been trying to write to you ever since Saturday and it was only stupid false pride that prevented me. It would have served me right if I'd lost you.

I don't agree that the blame was fifty-fifty, or anything like that. It was all my fault – but if it's any consolation to you, I've felt utterly miserable ever since.

I think you're wonderful, and I don't deserve you. Please come over as soon as you can for that make-up kiss.

Your loving
Beth

Letter from a man after a lovers' quarrel

137 Meadfoot Road
Bradley
Devon
BD22 1PT
9 July 19—

Darling

Will you forgive – and forget?

I was a fool last night and I know it. I can't imagine why I said what I did and I am kicking myself for being so stupid.

This is the first time we have quarrelled and I am determined that it will be the last. I've never felt so miserable in my life.

When may I come and see you again?

Your loving
Ed

Letter in reply to the previous example

68 Chesserton Road
Bradley
Devon
BD15 9XU
10 July 19—

My dearest Ed

It is forgotten as far as I am concerned. I don't need to forgive you, because you were not the only one to blame. It takes two to make a quarrel and I played my part too.

As you say, it was our first quarrel and I agree we should try to make it the last. I was feeling very miserable until your letter came.

Please come round as soon as you can.

Your loving
Pam

Letter from a mother to her son's fiancée

Ballington Grange
Denton
SE14 2TE
12 September 19—

My dear Patricia

Jack has written and told me of his great happiness in his engagement to you but I feel that I cannot properly share his feelings until I have met you and welcomed you as my new daughter.

Jack tells me that he can get away from work for a few days on the 28th, so I am writing to ask you whether you could come to stay with us then, so that we may all get to know you.

We should also like to meet your parents very soon.

Jack will only be able to stay for a few days but, if you would like to stay longer, we should be delighted to have you with us for the rest of the week.

Megan and Janet send their love and say they are most anxious to meet you, so do try to come.

I look forward to hearing from you.

Yours sincerely

Mary Woodrow

Letter written by a girl on being invited to visit her fiancé's family

14 Castle Street

Hendon

NW10 5BP

15 September 19—

My dear Mrs Woodrow

I think it is so very kind of you to write and ask me to visit you – I shall be pleased to come on the 28th, and I need not tell you how delighted I shall be to meet you.

Since I cannot take time off work at the moment, I will only be able to stay for two days, but I am sure that will give us the opportunity to begin to get to know each other.

Please give my love to Megan and Janet.

Yours sincerely

Patricia

Letter breaking off an engagement

36 Ditton Hill Lane
Charlton
Stafford
S15 9BQ
15 January 19—

Dear Harry

This is a very sad letter to have to write and you may be sure that I have given it many bitter hours, if not days or weeks, of consideration.

The fact is I have come to the conclusion that we are not right for each other and to marry in these circumstances would be quite wrong.

I think that the only sensible plan is for us to part and so I am writing to break off our engagement.

You have always been wonderful to me and I admire you tremendously; but, to be honest, I have come to feel that it is not love that has brought us together.

I know this will hurt you and it is hurting me to write it; but we must be sensible and face up to things as they really are. To continue would only make things more painful.

Yours sincerely
Diana

Letter from a man announcing his marriage

Knebworth
Clayton Hill
Hoddesdon
HO15 2DB
25 July 19—

Dear Ted

I feel like the happiest and luckiest man in the world. I am writing to tell you that I have just married the most wonderful girl on Earth.

I can imagine your smile at this – but you do not yet know from personal experience what is meant by 'the joys of matrimony'.

If you are in any way sceptical, come and see us very soon. Stay a day or two and we shall see if I can convince you of the reality of wedded bliss.

Mind you, I have very pleasant recollections of the many good times we had together in my bachelor days!

Kindest regards from Isabel,

> Yours ever
> Will

Letter congratulating a man on his marriage (1)

> Flat 23
> Savoy Court
> WC2 4YZ
> 29 July 19—

Dear Will

Your very welcome note, announcing your marriage, reached me this morning. I send you my hearty congratulations.

As I have not yet met the lady in question, I will take all you have said about her for granted.

I am delighted to accept your kind invitation, and you may expect to see me next Saturday.

My warmest regards to Isabel.

> Yours ever
> Ted

Letter congratulating a man on his marriage (2)

31 Selwyn Gardens
Blandford
BL15 2QP
16 April 19—

Dear Rupert

It seems that all the nice men are getting married and now I hear that you have joined the noble army. My mother and I wish you both a great deal of happiness and we send our congratulations.

We should love to meet Anna and so we hope you will bring her to see us one day very soon.

There is a small gift enclosed which Mother and I are sending with our best wishes to you both.

Yours sincerely
Harriet

Letter of thanks for a wedding present

Flat 15
38 Victoria Mansions
W21 5XR
18 June 19—

Dear Julia

It was very kind of you to send us such a lovely wedding present. I really don't know how to thank you. Derek was here last night and he is as pleased with it as I am.

We are looking forward to having you with us on the great day and, if you take my advice, you and Richard will follow our example very soon. I am terribly busy, but wonderfully happy.

Thank you very much.

Yours sincerely
Sally

Letter of congratulation on a silver wedding

14 Grant Street
Angmering
Sussex
AG4 3DT
10 June 19—

My dear Joe

It is just 25 years tomorrow since that memorable day when I played best man at your wedding. Afterwards I proposed the health of Mary and yourself and expressed the hope that you would have many happy years together.

Now you and Mary will be celebrating the occasion together, and you have every reason to feel pleased with yourselves. I know of only one other couple who have been as happy together as you – and you can guess whom I mean.

Joan joins me in wishing you many more years of happiness together. We enclose a little souvenir of the occasion – and I hope that we shall be able to send you another one in gold in 25 years' time.

Yours ever,
Tom

Letter in reply to the previous example

29 Neil Street
London
W4 5QR
14 June 19—

My dear Tom

How very kind of you to think of us on our silver wedding day. Your charming gift is in a place of honour on our sideboard – just next to the present you gave us 25 years ago, which has lasted as well as we have.

It was almost exactly three years after that day that I had the pleasure of being your best man, and I look forward to returning your congratulations when you join us in this silvered respectability.

Mary joins me in thanking you both and wishing you every happiness in the future.

Yours ever

Joe

Letter of congratulation on a golden wedding

The Haven

Seaburn

Dorset

SB5 7JN

3 November 19—

Dear Mr and Mrs Fox

Tomorrow is the fiftieth anniversary of your wedding day, and my wife and I wish to offer you our sincere congratulations.

No doubt you will be casting your minds back to various incidents in your married life and we are sure the thoughts will give you a great deal of pleasure. You have indeed had a fortunate time together, but that is only what you both deserve.

May life continue to be happy for you and may you both enjoy each other's company for many, many years to come.

Yours sincerely

Bill Thomas

· 4 ·

JOB APPLICATIONS AND EMPLOYMENT

Particularly in situations where there is intense competition, the letter you write to a prospective employer is absolutely vital in establishing the quality of your application. Make sure your letter is well presented, includes all the necessary information and is precise and to the point.

Curriculum vitae

Nowadays it is customary to enclose a curriculum vitae with a letter of application for a job. The object of the curriculum vitae, or CV as it is often called, is to set out clearly details of your education, qualifications and employment to date. You should also include your name, address, date of birth and the names of two people who have agreed to act as referees.

Always be as brief as possible; a CV should not be an account of your life. Try to include only information which is relevant to your application.

Example of a curriculum vitae (1)

Name:	Jane Brown
Address:	43 Chalcot Avenue London NW3 5DW
Telephone:	Home 0171 485 0387 Work 0171 822 3065
Date of birth:	22 August 1975
Marital status★:	Single
Secondary education:	Chillingford Green School, Chillingford, London, NW4 9DU
GCSEs passed:	English language (C) Mathematics (C) Geography (D) Textiles (B) French (D)
Employment record:	September 1992 to present Clerical assistant with Jacksons Limited, Greys Road, Chillingford, NW4 0PT

Referees:
Mr Stephen Taylor	Mrs Mary Morgan
Managing Director	Head teacher
Jacksons Limited	Chillingford Green School
London Road	Chillingford
Chillingford,	NW4 9DU
NW4 0PT	

★ *You are not obliged to give your marital status and employers are legally bound not to take this into account when recruiting staff.*

Example of a curriculum vitae (2)

Name: Jane Brown

Address: 43 Chalcot Avenue
                               London
                               NW3 5DW

Telephone: Home 0171 485 0387
                               Work 0171 822 3065

Date of birth: 8 August 1948

Secondary education: 1966-69 Manchester University
                               BA (Second Class Honours) in History

                               1959-66 St Marks School for Girls
                               6 O-levels passed
                               3 A-levels
                               History Grade B
                               Geography Grade C
                               Latin Grade C

Employment to date:

1975-present   Area Manager (Marketing) with Framley
                 (UK) Ltd, Hope House, Thorpe Way,
                 Onsworth, DJ2 2PT

1971-75   Assistant Manager (Sales) Unitech Limited as
                 above

1970-71   Management trainee with Unitech Limited,
                 Unitech House, Queen Street, Onsworth,
                 DB6 6TZ

Referees: Mr K. Parks   Mr B. Crane
              Department of History   Managing Director
              Manchester   Framley (UK) Ltd
              M14 3DU   Thorpe Way
                                          Onsworth
                                          DJ2 2PT

Application for a job as a typist

38 West Park Terrace
Hamford
DW15 5PU
3 September 19—

The Office Manager
Atlas Glassworks Ltd
15 Dean Street
Hamford
DW15 2XW

Dear Sir

I write in answer to your advertisement for a typist in this morning's *Daily Telegraph*.

I am 18 years of age and have just left the ... School. I have GCSE passes in Mathematics, English Language, French, Art and Geography. I have good keyboard skills and can take shorthand at 100 WPM.

I should be pleased to attend for an interview at any time, and I am enclosing the names and addresses of two referees.

Yours faithfully
Susan Hellier (Miss)
Encs.

Naturally, as the post is for a typist, the letter submitted must be a perfect example of typing.

Application for a business post

77 **Gerald Crescent**
Somerleigh
Maidstone
MD13 2UQ
18 July 19—

The Personnel Manager
The Empire Trading Concern
10 High Street
Rotherham
RH10 9DN

Dear Sir

I wish to apply for the post which you have advertised as vacant in today's *Daily Telegraph.*

I enclose a summary of my qualifications and experience, together with the names of two referees.

In particular, I should like to draw your attention to .... *(place here any special qualifications).*

I should be pleased to come for an interview at almost any time by appointment.

Yours faithfully
G. Williams
Encs.

Application for a junior post in an office

13 Valley Road
Beechcroft
Surrey
3 October 19—

The Office Manager
Messrs Axford & Co. Ltd

Dear Sir,

I understand that you have a vacancy in your office for a junior clerk and would like to offer myself for the post.

At present I am a pupil in the sixth form of the County School, Beechcroft, and I want to go into a business career.

Last summer, I obtained passes in six subjects at GCSE and my headmaster tells me that he will be able to answer favourably any questions regarding my character. I am 17 years of age.

I should be pleased to come for an interview whenever it is convenient to you.

Yours faithfully
R.G. Norman

Response to an advertisement about a vacant post

33 Ferndale Mansions
Ealing
W5 9DE
8 July 19—

Box 354
c/o *The Daily Journal*

Dear Sir

In answer to your advertisement in *The Daily Journal* of today's date, I wish to offer myself for the vacant post.

I am enclosing my CV which gives details of my experience and qualifications which, I think, will help you most in considering my application. But I should like to mention specially that I ....

I should be glad to come for an interview at any time which is convenient to you.

Yours faithfully
G. Gregory
Encs.

Fill in the blank space with details of some special qualifications and do not forget to enclose the additional sheet with full particulars in column form.

Letter applying for a post

68 Middleford Road
Templeton
TE3 4DP
16 March 19—

G.A. Barrow Esq.
The Tile and Timber Works
Templeton
TE1 5QR

Dear Sir

I wish to enquire as to whether you have a vacancy for a .... Mr Arthur Burton, who is a mutual friend, has suggested that I write to you as he informs me that you have recently been expanding your workforce.

Until two months ago, I was a .... at the Crown Works, but as you may be aware that factory has recently closed down I have been unemployed, despite actively seeking work during that time.

Mr Burton has kindly agreed to provide a character reference for me and I should be pleased to come for an interview.

I look forward to hearing from you.

Yours faithfully
A. Page

Reply to an invitation to an interview

68 Middleford Road
Templeton
TE3 4DP
20 March 19—

G.A. Barrow Esq.
The Tile and Timber Works
Templeton
TE1 5QR

Dear Sir

Thank you for your letter of March 19th, in which you invite me to call for an interview.

I shall be pleased to attend, as directed, on Thursday March 24th at 3.15 p.m.

Yours faithfully
A. Page

It is very important that such a letter should be sent. First, it shows that the one seeking the post pays attention to details; it reminds the receiver of the engagement, and it effectively checks any mistake that could be made about the time and the date.

Application for a job as sales representative

Hollydene
Collingwood Road
Norton
DH4 5UT
27 August 19—

Box 3998
The Daily Mercury

Dear Sirs

I should like to apply for the post advertised in this morning's *Daily Mercury*.

I am 26 years of age and in good health.

I have worked as a representative for ...., covering the .... area.

My present line is ....

My weekly turnover, at present, averages ....

I enclose my CV, giving full details of my qualifications and work record to date.

Yours faithfully,
B. Gray
Encs.

Applications, such as this, which are crisp and to the point often draw attention when longer and more involved ones are passed over.

Letter offering to act as an agent

167 Grove Avenue
Broomfields
York
YK6 4DL
19 November 19—

Messrs Roberts and Perry Ltd
23 Broomhouse Drive
Birmingham
B14 9LD

Dear Sirs

Every week I have to call on 50 confectioners in the Northern Counties. I am told that you have no representatives in this area. As your lines do not in any way compete with those which I currently promote, I could represent your goods to our mutual advantage.

Would you be interested in appointing me as your representative for this area?

Yours faithfully
S. Cathcart

Application for a job as a store cashier

38 Fallowfield Road
Litchfield
NW30 2BQ
3 August 19—

The Manager
Messrs Stoker & Co. Ltd

Dear Sir

I wish to apply for the post of store cashier, which you are advertising as vacant in *The Daily Post*.

At present, I am cashier in the hardware department of Messrs. Timson's Store. I am 21 years of age and earning £ ... per week. My reason for applying to you is that you are offering a higher wage and better prospects.

I am a quick and accurate worker and I have only had three days' absence in the last three and a half years.

I enclose a testimonial written by my present manager.

Yours faithfully
Jane Jeavons (Miss)
Encs.

Application for a post in a chain store

538 Pemberton Road
New Southgate
N11 4WR
30 October 19—

Box 398
The Morning Argus

Dear Sir

I have read your advertisement in today's *Morning Argus* and wish to apply for one of the vacant posts of sales assistant which you mention.

I have had five years' sales experience in two different firms. Although I have worked mainly in small retail outlets, I think my experience would be valuable in the position you describe.

I am very keen to secure a post which would give full scope for my energies, and offer me opportunities for further career development.

Yours faithfully
S. Beechcroft (Mrs)
Encs.

Letter refusing a job offer

3 Streatley Road
Sydenham Rise
SE13 5RX
18 January 19—

George Barker Esq.
The Towers
Beckenham
Kent

Dear Sir

Thank you for offering me the vacant post of chauffeur.

By a strange coincidence, I was today offered a similar position at a higher wage. I feel it a duty to my family that I should accept the better wage, and I have done so.

Therefore, it is with regret that I must withdraw my application to you, but I thank you, none the less.

Yours faithfully
James Hogg

Letter taking up a reference

The Loughton Works
Muchford
Hants
MC3 1FX
18 July 19—

Messrs Mayford & Co. Ltd
Southampton SO5 4DW

Dear Sirs

We have just had an interview with Mr Arthur Meyrick, who has applied for the post of cashier with us.

He has given your name as a referee, stating that he has served you for three years in a similar capacity.

Would you be so kind as to send us a note stating whether you consider him a suitable man to appoint? Any information you may be able to give us will be valued and treated in confidence.

Yours faithfully
G.R. Rhead (Director)

Letter of reference

Mayford & Co. Ltd
Southampton
SO5 4DW
26 July 19—

G.R. Rhead Esq.
The Loughton Works
Muchford
Hants
MC3 1FX

Dear Sir

In reply to your letter of July 18th, I have been asked by our Managing Director to inform you that Mr Arthur Meyrick has worked here a cashier for a period of three years.

During this time he has proved himself to be efficient and capable, and his only reason for wishing to leave us is to seek a more remunerative post.

Should he be successful in his application to you, our company will be sorry to lose his services; but, at the same time, we would wish him well in his new position.

Yours faithfully
S.G. Smith (Director)

Letter asking for a reference

48 Cambridge Road
High End
Lexford
LX14 9DB
4 September 19—

Dear Mr Browning

When I left school at the end of last term, you very kindly suggested that I might use your name when seeking a post. I am applying for the position of .... in the Anglo-French Oil Company and have given your name as one of three referees.

I understand the company may write to you and, if so, I hope you will be happy to write a favourable reference for me. The post is not a highly paid one, but it offers excellent prospects.

I should like to take this opportunity of thanking you for all you did for me while I was at school.

Yours sincerely
N. Scott

It is a matter of courtesy to tell the recipient that his or her name has been used as a reference.

Letter giving a reference for a domestic help

3 Bishop's Walk
Hampton
TW5 4XM
3 January 19—

Dear Mrs Larcombe

In reply to your letter, dated January 1st, I have much pleasure in recommending Joan Brasset. She was with me for three years and left last June when her mother became ill. She has a pleasant manner and is perfectly trustworthy and extremely thoughtful.

Were I coming back to London, I should be quite prepared to re-engage her.

Yours faithfully
Nancy French

The chief thing to avoid when writing a reference is excessive praise. When overdone, it is liable to have an adverse effect.

Letter regarding a job as a nanny

Norfolk Lodge
Billington
Lincolnshire
LN7 9RS
6 May 19—

Dear Madam

Thank you for your reply to my advertisement for post as a nanny. In my present post, which I am leaving next month, I have had sole charge of four children since the birth of the youngest little girl, who is now five years old.

There are three other children, a boy aged six and a half and twins, a boy and a girl aged eight, and as they are all now of school age, their mother, Lady Charles, has decided that she does not require a full-time nanny but intends to employ an au pair instead.

I am 32 years old and, as you can imagine, I am very fond of children, having worked with them throughout my career. My last post, where I stayed three years, was also as nanny to a family of four children.

My present salary is £ ..., with an allowance of £ ... for expenses. Lady Charles has kindly offered to write a reference for me and I can provide others if you require them.

Would you be so kind as to let me know as soon as possible if you wish to interview me as I have had other answers to my advertisement.

Yours faithfully
Marion Russell

Letter enquiring about the character of a nanny

Brussington Hall
Northborough
NT5 6LU
8 May 19—

Dear Lady Charles

I am considering employing Marion Russell as nanny to my three small children who are at present aged ten months, two and four years.

Miss Russell states that she has been in full charge of your children for five years and that they have been happy and healthy throughout that time. I should like to know whether you would agree with this and whether you consider her to be reliable and trustworthy.

I should be pleased to have any information you think may be useful to me in considering her for the post and would be grateful if you could indicate whether you would recommend her to me as nanny to my children.

Yours sincerely
Joan Foskett

Letter accepting a post

51 St Paul's Road
London
EC4 8HY
18 October 19—

Mr R. Burns
Director, Human Resources
Timetec Ltd
Rose Estate
Oxridge
Bucks
SL9 5RF

Dear Mr Burns

Thank you for your letter of 12th October offering me the post of office administrator with your organisation.

I am delighted to accept the position and look forward to starting work with you on 15th November.

Yours sincerely
Jane Allcock

Letter of resignation

3 Ham Terrace
Hamborough
Lincolnshire
LN4 7XG
15 August 19—

G.A. Lindsey Esq.
Messrs Lindsey & Co. Ltd

Dear Sir

I have recently accepted a post with Messrs Smith and Taylor Ltd, of Merrowbridge and start work there early in October.

I am therefore writing to give you the appropriate notice to terminate my employment with your company on September 16th.

I should like to take this opportunity of thanking you for all your consideration in the past five years.

I shall be sorry to leave but the new post carries with it greater responsibilities, and I feel that they will help to advance me in my career.

Yours faithfully
B. Mansbridge

This letter is suitable when the writer is leaving in an amicable manner.

Letter of resignation (short)

3 Ham Terrace
Hamborough
Lincolnshire
15 August 19—

Messrs Lindsey & Co. Ltd

Dear Sirs

I wish to offer you my resignation, to take effect on September 16th 19—.

Yours faithfully
B. Mansbridge

Such a letter is only suitable when the writer wishes to resign in a dignified manner, but has a grievance of some sort. Many people would be tempted to add a few lines of abuse but in the long run the above is much better.

Letter confirming an arrangement for flexible working hours

18 Hetherington Close
Birmingham
B2 7FG
21 January 19—

Mr M. Jones
Human Resources Manager
Magitech Limited

Dear Mr Jones

Thank you so much for taking the time to talk to me yesterday and for your kind suggestions to solve my present difficulties with my elderly mother and my children.

I now wish to confirm that I would be most willing to try the flexible working arrangements that you offered. The later start and finish times will be more convenient for my home circumstances.

It may also be helpful for you to know that I have at home my own word processor which is compatible with those we use at Magitech. If there is an emergency at home and I have to leave early, I would be very happy to complete any unfinished work during the evenings or at weekends. Please let me know if this suggestion meets with your approval.

Yours sincerely
Annette Hobbs

Letter asking for an increased salary

27 Kinsbridge Mansions
Putney
SW15 9WW
28 October 19—

R. Fullerton Esq.
Messrs Fullerton & Sons Ltd
Crawley Road
Sutton
SN3 5LW

Dear Sir

I am writing to ask if you could consider the question of my salary.

During the last two years I have not had an increase, though I think you will agree that many responsibilities have been added to my work during this period.

I am very happy in the office and like my work, but with the ever-increasing expenditure of a growing family, I find it difficult to balance my budget.

I should appreciate the opportunity to discuss this with you further.

Yours faithfully
G.S. Blackman

Letter to a Citizens Advice Bureau, asking about maternity leave regulations

45 Maple Road
Sheffield
S12 7VT
29 July 19—

Citizens Advice Bureau
17 High Street
Sandwich
Kent
SD4 9TH

Dear Sirs

Re: Maternity Leave Regulations

I should like some information on the above. I am single, aged 30, and have worked for the last three years as a waitress at Corkers Wine Bar. I am three months pregnant but have not yet told my employer because I am afraid I shall lose my job.

Could you please let me know what protection I have under present regulations?

I am sorry that I cannot call at your office in person because of the hours I work, but I should be grateful for any advice you may be able to give me.

Yours faithfully
Ann Blunt

The Citizens Advice Bureau can give information and advice on many aspects of employment law. You will find their address in your local telephone directory.

Letter requesting holiday entitlement

10 Vicarage Lane
Oxford
OX12 3RT
23 January 19—

Mr F. Brown
Human Resources
Technofit Ltd

Dear Mr Brown

I would like to take two weeks of my holiday entitlement for this year (19—) from 6–19 June inclusive and the other two weeks from 9–22 September inclusive.

Please confirm this as soon as possible.

Yours sincerely
Alan Jones

· 5 ·

FAMILY MATTERS

Letters dealing with what are essentially family matters come within this section. But the sections on Money and Home, Domestic Matters, Invitations and Replies, etc. contain many letters that also apply to home matters.

Letter requesting a school prospectus

34 King Edward Mews
Windsor
SL4 9IK
31 May 19—

The Secretary
Peveril Hill School
Stanton
Hants
GH9 7TW

Dear Madam

We shall shortly be moving to Stanton and are therefore looking for a suitable school for our daughters, aged 12 and 14. Peveril Hill School has been highly praised by our friends, Mr and Mrs John Bloggs, whose daughter Patricia is a pupil at present.

I should be pleased if you would send me a prospectus of the school, together with any information you have about arrangements for visitors.

Yours faithfully
Gerald Gray

Letter putting a child's name down for school

24 Northwood Avenue
Bristol
BS4 8TF
29 September 19—

Dr W.R. Weston
Headteacher
Shipley Court Preparatory School
Fawley Lane
Long Melford
Suffolk
GU12 4ST

Dear Dr Weston

Our son Mark was born on 28th June of this year and I am writing to register his name for entrance as a boarding pupil at Shipley Court for the year starting September 19—.

As you know, I attended Shipley Court myself, as did my father, and I consider that the educational and sporting facilities it offers are quite exceptional.

We should prefer Mark to join Askins, my old house.

My best wishes to Mrs Weston.

Yours sincerely
Peter M. Hayward

Letter regarding the absence of a child from school

80 Fulwell Road
Fulham
SW6 4XB
3 March 19—

The Headteacher
St Mary's Junior School
Hill Green
Fulham

Dear Madam

My daughter Susan is returning to school today, after nearly a week's absence. She has been suffering from a chest infection and so it seemed advisable to keep her at home.

She is much better now and I will encourage her to do what she can to make up for lost time.

Yours faithfully
Jean Wormald

Letter asking for a child's homework to be excused

66 Goldsmith Road
Highfields
Westerham
Kent
WH2 9VL
19 February 19—

The Headteacher
Westerham Middle School
Westerham

Dear Madam★

I am sorry that Barbara was unable to do her homework last night.

Unfortunately, she came home at teatime with a bad headache and as I thought it necessary for her to go to bed she was unable to do the work set.

Yours faithfully*
Mary Simmonds

If preferred, substitute the name of the headteacher, and write 'Yours sincerely'.

Letter requesting a child be excused from religious instruction

15 Woodside Close
Berryford
Sussex
SN3 3II
21 April 19—

Miss S. Butcher
Headteacher
Berryford School
Berryford
Sussex
SN3 4PD

Dear Miss Butcher

Our son Sikander is to be a pupil at your school from September of this year and I am taking this opportunity to request that he be excused from religious instruction.

Although he was born in this country, he has been raised in the Sikh faith and receives instruction according to our own religion.

Yours sincerely
Dilip Patel

Letter complaining about bullying in school

2 School Lane
Bayford
EP4 9NB
27 February 19—

Mr P. Bowlson
Headteacher
Highfield School
Dean Road
Bayford
Essex
EP4 1SD

Dear Mr Bowlson

I wish to inform you of a very serious situation involving our daughter Susan. It appears she has been the victim of a group of older girls who pick on the most junior pupils and demand money from them. When my daughter refused to hand over the small amount of money she had, she was verbally abused and even punched and kicked.

Susan is not the sort of child to tell tales and normally looks after herself, but this does seem to be a particularly nasty form of bullying. She does not know the names of the girls involved except for one, Karen Wilcox, who appears to be the ringleader.

As today is Friday, I am keeping Susan at home. She is still very upset, and has some visible bruises. I shall telephone you on Monday morning when you will have received this letter. I hope that you will be able to assure me that this unacceptable behaviour will be stopped immediately and the culprits punished in an appropriate manner.

Yours sincerely
Carol Potter (Mrs)

Letter removing a child from school

19 Hazel Street
Grazeley
TW14 5TF
16 October 19—

Miss M. Metcalfe
Headteacher
Hampton Park School
Grazeley
Middx
TW14 3RR

Dear Miss Metcalfe

I wish to inform you that our daughter, Rachel, will be leaving Hampton Park at the end of this term.

My husband's company has relocated to Berkshire and Rachel will be attending Middle Hill School, just outside Newbury, which I understand has an excellent academic record.

Thank you for all the encouragement you and your staff have given to Rachel during the last two years.

Yours sincerely
Elizabeth Walters (Mrs)

Letter apologising for a late reply

Mayfields
River Lane
Salisbury
S23 4WN
6 February 19—

Dear Diana

I owe you a very sincere apology. You wrote to me some weeks ago, and up till now your letter has remained unanswered. I don't usually make excuses, but on this occasion, I think I should explain what happened.

When your letter arrived ....
....
....
In your letter, you asked ....
....
....

In the circumstances, I do hope you will accept my apology and forgive me for my apparent rudeness.

Yours sincerely
Penny Appleton

In the first space, give some reason for the delay in answering, such as absence from home, illness, loss of the address, etc.

Letter congratulating a friend on passing her examinations

71 Hill Crescent
Cambridge
CA5 4HB
1 July 19—

Dear Emily

I have just heard that you have passed your examinations with flying colours. Congratulations! You ought to be proud of such an achievement. You certainly deserved to get through, for if anyone worked hard, it was you.

My mother is also singing your praises: she says your parents must be proud of you and she says she wishes she had a daughter like you. I am afraid, however, that I was not built that way but it doesn't stop me from being pleased for you.

I hope you are now having a good rest – you certainly deserve it.

Yours ever
Pamela

Letter of thanks for being taken out (from a child)

38 Cantrell Avenue
Sidford
Surrey
SD2 9NY
8 July 19—

Dear Uncle Bob,

I am writing to tell you how much I enjoyed myself the day before yesterday. You gave me a really exciting time and I think I was very lucky.

What I liked most was ....; but it was great to have dinner (tea) with you in a lovely restaurant. In fact, the whole day was good.

Thank you very much.

Love from
Phillip

Letter of thanks (from an adult)

38 Cantrell Avenue
Sidford
Surrey
SD2 9NY
16 May 19—

Dear Juliet,

Just a note to tell you how much I enjoyed last Tuesday evening and to thank you for taking me to the ....

For a long time I have wanted to see it (or go there) and now I feel I have achieved one of my ambitions.

I never was a great one for going to things by myself and I appreciated your company very much.

It was a really enjoyable evening.

Yours sincerely,
Joan Boardman

'Thank you' letter (from a child)

539 Ellerton Drive
Leeds
L15 9XR
27 December 19—

Dear Mrs Thompson

I had a nice lot of Christmas presents — cassettes, several books, some paints and your chemistry set. How did you know that I wanted one? It was just what I wanted, as nearly all my friends at school have them. I have made up a lot of chemicals with it already and I had a particularly good time with the invisible ink!

I hope Tom had a nice lot of presents and that he enjoyed Christmas as much as I did.

Yours sincerely,
Michael

Letter of thanks (from a parent for a baby's gift)

62 Kennedy Road
Bracknell
RG40 6BQ
6 January 19—

Dear Steve and Claire

Thank you very much for Harry's Christmas present. It was sweet of you to think of him and I can tell you that he is having a great time with it. He seems to have a musical inclination already, so a toy xylophone was the perfect present for him — although our ears are suffering!

We had a wonderful first Christmas with Harry — you were right, the family atmosphere does make the occasion.

I will be in touch again soon but, in the meantime, many thanks again.

With love,
Liz, Allan and Harry

Letter Asking a Friend to be Executor of a Will

54 Blackhorse Avenue
Cottenham
Cambs
CA6 2NR
8 July 19—

Dear Mr Wallis

I want to ask a favour and I sincerely hope you will be able to help me.

I am about to make my will and I think you would be well qualified to perform the part of Executor. Therefore, may I fill in your name as Executor on my will?

I know it is a thankless task, but if you said yes it would go a long way towards setting my mind at rest.

Yours sincerely,
S. Watson

(An executor should, properly, be someone who has every expectation of being alive and active when the person who makes the will dies.)

· 6 ·

BUSINESS
MATTERS

The letters in this chapter cover a range of business circumstances and should prove particularly useful to people with small businesses or people who work from an office at home.

Letter of enquiry about the price of goods

769 Burdett Road
Bristol
BS8 1JW
8 March 19—

Messrs John Mathers & Son
17 Broad Street
Leeds
L7 9QB

Dear Sirs

I am informed that you are manufacturers of .... If this is the case, will you please let me know if you can supply me with the following items, and quote your best trade terms?

....
....

Delivery will be required within two months of date of order.

Yours faithfully
George Brown

Letter of acknowledgement

Glaslyn
Cumberland Drive
Beechford
BD5 2JL
8 March 19—

Messrs Wilcox & Jones Ltd
21 Princes Street
Gloucester
G2 4RM

Dear Sirs

I acknowledge receipt of your letter of 4th March which is receiving my attention.

I hope to give you a definite answer within the next week.

Yours faithfully
R. Goodyear

Letter apologising for not being able to keep a business appointment

51 Goldheron Road
Shepherd's Bush
SW15 2JL
30 June 19—

B. Martin Esq.
29 Shere Place
Reigate
RG4 2QN

Dear Sir

Since my letter to you of 24th June, circumstances have arisen which mean I shall be out of the country during the next ten days; I shall therefore be unable to keep my appointment with you as arranged on 1st July.

I am sorry to postpone our meeting, but after the 6th July, I shall be free to meet you at a date and time convenient to you.

Yours faithfully
L. Seers

Letter apologising to a customer for a delay in supplying goods

M. Taylor Ltd
West Close Business Units
Marford
BL3 2NL
16 July 19—

E. Fyfield Esq.
3 Collerton Drive
Marford
BL6 2RQ

Dear Sir

We much regret that we have been unable to complete your order by the date promised.

Unfortunately, we have experienced considerable difficulty in obtaining spare parts. The position has now, however, improved a little and we are making every effort to deliver the goods with the least possible delay.

A consignment of .... will be forwarded to you tomorrow, and the balance will be finished by 10th June at the latest.

As the circumstances have been altogether beyond our control, we hope you will accept this explanation and arrangement.

Yours faithfully
M. Taylor Ltd

Letter apologising to a customer for not being able to supply goods ordered

Butler and Butler Ltd
91–3 Granby Road
Littleton
HA3 9XY
8 August 19—

Mrs B. Thomas
The Vicarage
Littleton
HA3 4PG

Dear Madam

With reference to your letter of 12th July, and our reply, we regret to inform you it will not be possible to supply the articles you require within the time specified. Those firms which we believed to be manufacturers of these articles inform us that they are no longer made in this country. Please accept our apologies for misinforming you.

In the meantime we are enclosing some samples, which although not exactly the same as your sample, may be near enough to suit your needs. We can supply them at ... and can deliver immediately.

Assuring you of our best attention,

Yours faithfully
Butler and Butler Ltd

Letter asking for a bill to be paid

37 West Street
Marlton
Bucks
SL7 2NB
15 September 19—

E. Wolverton Esq.
3 Market Place
Billingsden
BN2 5RT

Dear Sir

A statement of our account was forwarded to you on 10th August. We have not received a remittance, but it is possible our letter has been mislaid.

Will you kindly let us know whether this is the case, so that we may then supply a copy?

Yours faithfully
Frank Acton & Co.

Letter pressing for a bill to be paid

37 West Street
Marlton
Bucks
SL7 2NB
15 September 19—

E. Wolverton Esq.
3 Market Place
Billingsden
BN2 5RT

Dear Sir

We much regret that we must draw your attention once more to the account forwarded to you on 10th August.

Payment is now four weeks overdue and we must ask that you will be good enough to make a settlement by return of post.

Yours faithfully
Frank Acton & Co.

Letter threatening proceedings

50 Roman Terrace
Chalk Farm
NW1 9DP
16 July 19—

A. Campion Esq.
2 High Street
Finchley
NW7 2PN

Dear Sir

Unless your account is settled within the next seven days, I shall be reluctantly obliged to place the matter in the hands of my solicitor.

Yours faithfully
F. Putnam

It is important to note that a private person must not threaten proceedings in a definite way. Only a solicitor may do that.

Letter requesting settlement of an account

Eastwood Stores
High Street
Littlefield Green
HG10 7NW
28th December 19—

M. Price Esq.
17 Coronation Road
Littlefield Green
HG10 5RZ

Dear Sir

We shall be greatly obliged if you could send us a cheque for the goods supplied to you during October and November 19—.

Our accounts are balanced during the first week of January in each year and the delay in receiving your settlement is preventing us from closing our books.

A duplicate invoice is enclosed.

Yours faithfully
pp The Eastwood Stores
S.F. Fothergill

A strong letter requesting settlement of an account

Eastwood Stores
High Street
Littlefield Green
HG10 7NW
15th January 19—

M. Price Esq.
17 Coronation Road
Littlefield Green
HG10 5RZ

Dear Sir

We regret to note that the account for goods supplied during October and November of last year is still outstanding.

We have already written to you several times regarding the matter and have sent duplicate invoices.

In the circumstances, we regret to have to inform you that, unless we receive a settlement in the next seven days, we shall be obliged to instruct our solicitors to institute proceedings against you.

Yours faithfully
pp The Eastwood Stores
S.F. Fothergill

Note: The abbreviation pp stands for per pro and indicates that the letter has been signed by someone other than the writer whose name appears at the end.

It is not wise to send such a letter unless proceedings are really intended.

Letter to a creditor who is pressing for payment

79 Redbridge Road
Axford
Herts
AX9 6DU
8 July 19—

S. Jefferson Esq.
Axford Motor Supplies
Axford
AX2 5RY

Dear Sir

I have received your warning of legal proceedings with regard to our outstanding account. I am sorry that you are considering such drastic action.

I am as anxious as you to settle the account, but I have to inform you that I am unable to pay at the present time. However, I am confident that I shall be able to do so at the beginning of next month.

I sincerely regret the delay which has occurred, but trust that we may continue to do business.

Yours faithfully
John Birch

Letter to a creditor pressing for payment

79 Redbridge Road
Axford
Herts
AX9 6DU
8 July 19—

S. Jefferson Esq.
Axford Motor Supplies
Axford
AX2 5RY

Dear Sir

I was very surprised to receive this morning your letter threatening legal proceedings if I do not forward a full remittance within six days.

I deeply regret that you should consider such a step necessary. I have dealt with you for over two years, and that during that time I have always settled my monthly accounts very promptly.

Proceedings would put both of us to unnecessary trouble, without improving the position. As an old customer, I hope you will reconsider the matter, and be good enough to allow me a little grace.

I am forwarding a small remittance on account, as evidence of my good faith and would be pleased to discuss arrangements for the balance.

Yours faithfully
John Birch

Letter requesting a final account

1 Victory Lane
Twynham
DW14 9DR
15 May 19—

M. Taylor Esq.
Twynham Garden Services
Orchard Hill
Twynham
DW14 6PN

Dear Mr Taylor

I am moving away from the district in a few weeks' time, and would ask you to send your account to me, so that I may settle it before leaving.

I should like to thank you for the service you have given my family and myself, which I am sure will be sadly missed.

Yours sincerely
F. Carey

Letter requesting a statement of account

Alloa Road
Newington
Kent
NT2 4QR
11 August 19—

Messrs Perkins & Lambton Ltd
High Street
Newington
NT1 9PF

Dear Sirs

I should be obliged if you would forward to me, at your

earliest convenience, your statement of account up to and including the 31st ult.

Yours faithfully
S. Warwick

Ult. [ultimo], meaning last, prox. [proximo], meaning next and inst. [instant], meaning present, all refer to the month in the date. In this example, 31st ult. means 31st July. These abbreviations are old-fashioned, however, and rarely used nowadays.

Letter pointing out an error in a statement received

Alloa Road
Newington
Kent
NT2 4QR
15 August 19—

Messrs Perkins & Lambton Ltd
High Street
Newington
NT1 9PF

Dear Sirs

I have received your statement of yesterday's date. Before settling, however, I must point out that item 4, in respect of ...., does not agree with your quotation submitted to me on 6th July. Also, you have omitted to credit me with the value of the goods returned on 10th July, for which I hold your carrier's receipt.

When I have received an amended statement, I will forward to you my cheque in full settlement.

Yours faithfully
S. Warwick

Letter complaining of an overcharge in an invoice

168 Avenue Road
Highford
Bucks
HP3 4DY
8 January 19—

Paul Jones & Co. Ltd
Station Road
Highford
HP3 9XY

Dear Sirs

I am in receipt of your invoice dated January 1st. As you will notice, the second item is for ...... goods at a cost of £1.25. These were sent with the original order, but were returned by me because ....

I am returning your invoice and, when it has been amended, I shall be pleased to forward you my cheque.

Yours faithfully
R. Simpson

Letter accompanying an estimate

68 Globe Villas
Wallerton
Salisbury
S23 6VU
11 April 19—

G. Smithers Esq.
18 Somerfield Drive
Salisbury
S5 8JK

Dear Sir

A few days ago you were good enough to ask me to give you an estimate for certain repairs.

I have carefully checked over the work and now have pleasure in submitting the estimate. I may add that the figure quoted is for best materials and workmanship.

Hoping that my quotation will prove acceptable,

Yours faithfully
N. Fitzwilliam

Letter asking for a cheque to be redated

7 The Treeway
Portaton
Somerset
T53 6DU
8 July 19—

The Secretary
Anglo-Australian Timbers Ltd
Cambridge Drive
Portaton
T53 2DY

Dear Sir

I am enclosing a cheque for £15 which you sent me a little over two months ago. Unfortunately, it has been mislaid until now and my bank will not accept it, as it bears a note to the effect that it must be passed for payment within one month.

In the circumstances I should be very much obliged if you would help me to secure payment.

Yours faithfully
A. Dutt

Wording to use on a promissory note

65 Easterham Road
Broughton
Kent
BT6 2XS
15 June 19—

£100

STAMP

Three months after date, I promise to pay to F.R. Taylor Esq., or order, the sum of one hundred pounds sterling for value received.

John Heathcote

Wording for a joint promissory note

23 Heath Road
Dunston
Sussex
DT4 3LW
15 June 19—

£400

STAMP

Six months after date, we promise to pay F.R. Taylor Esq., or order, the sum of four hundred pounds sterling for value received.

James Fleming
Arthur Alexander

Wording to use on an IOU

31 Queens Court
St Pauls
Birmingham
B3 1RD
18 May 19—

To Matthew Duncan Esq.
IOU One Hundred Pounds
£100

John Archer Smith

*No stamp is required; but if any additional wording is used to suggest
a promise of paying, then the document has the effect of a promissory
note and needs a stamp.*

Example of a receipt

75 Frith Road
Nottingham

Received from Richard Shipman, the sum of eight hundred
and seventy five pounds only, in payment for Vauxhall van,
registration number C365 NYO, delivered to him on 3rd
April 19—.

(sign)
Brian Hicks
3 April 19—

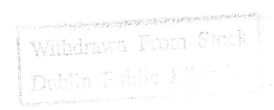

Example of an invoice

Pennine Motors Limited
Bowater Street
York
YO8 9TF
Vat Reg No 593 5739

27

19 November 19—

Invoice No 76

To:
A.P. Smith and Sons
49 London Road
Arbroath
AR9 7GD

Sale Quantity	Description	Price Excl. VAT	VAT
1	Exhaust Pipe	£50.00	£8.75
2	Brackets	£20.00	£3.50
		£70.00	£12.25

Total Price £82.25

Terms: 30 days nett
Cash discount of 5% if paid within 14 days

Example of a statement

Pennine Motors
Bowater Street
York
YO8 9TF
19 November 19—

Statement of Account

A.P. Smith and Sons
49 London Road
Arbroath
AR9 7GD

Date of sale	Reference	Amount
06.09.96	48200 CSH	29.75
16.10.96	48309 INV	43.96
21.10.96	48750 INV	8.44
23.10.96	48964 INV	18.94

Balance outstanding £41.59

INV	–	invoice
CSH	–	payment received
CR	–	credit

· 7 ·

CLUBS AND SOCIETIES

Organising the activities of a club or society, however small, can be time-consuming and may require considerable diplomacy. The letters in this chapter may help anyone involved in such a task.

Letter to a person who wishes to become a member

Four Winds Golf Club
Hatherway
Sussex
HY2 7GC
15 July 19—

Dr A. Grant
Victoria Road
Hatherway
HY4 8MG

Dear Sir

I have been asked to inform you that at a meeting of the Four Winds Golf Club, held in the clubhouse on June 30th, your name was submitted to the members.

I am pleased to report that you were unanimously elected a member of the club.

I enclose forms 3 and 4, which I shall be pleased if you would complete and return to me, at your convenience.

Yours faithfully
A.R. Bowley (Secretary)

Letter of reminder that a subscription is due

The Castleways
Shirley upon Avon
Gloucestershire
ST4 9DB
1 April 19—

Miss N. Harket
Caversham Drive
Shirley upon Avon
ST9 2LU

Dear Madam

I have to inform you that the annual subscription of £20 to the Castleways Tennis Club is now due.

I shall be pleased to receive your cheque before the end of this month.

Yours faithfully
Catherine Burke (Secretary)

Letter requesting payment of an overdue subscription

The Three Turrets
Borsfield
Kent
BR9 2ZD
10 August 19—

Miss R. Plunkett
The Old Rectory
Borsfield
BR5 4CH

Dear Madam

I regret to note that your subscription to the Victoria Tennis Club is still outstanding. By the club's rules (No. 7), all subscriptions are due on January 1st of each year and no member is allowed to play on the courts after August 1st if their subscription is still unpaid.

In the circumstances, I should be glad if you could forward to me your cheque for £20 by return.

Yours faithfully
M. Jessop

Letter about the formation of a local society

The Homestead
Ditchford
DD2 7MH
2 March 19—

Miss T. Harley
Post Office Cottage
Ditchford
DD4 6VN

Dear Miss Harley

At an informal meeting held here last evening, it was decided to consider instituting a local literary and debating society.

It was proposed to hold an open meeting to discuss the matter at the Lopping Hall, next Wednesday, March 8th, at 7.15 p.m.

Knowing that you are interested in local affairs of this nature, I wonder if you would like to attend?

We believe there is a great need for such a society and many residents will, we hope, enjoy the social opportunities which it will offer them.

Yours sincerely
S. Blandford

Letter announcing a society meeting

Oakdene
Pershore Road
Stamford
SM2 5NV

E. Turner Esq.
17 Long Lane
Stamford
SM11 2XT

Dear Sir

I wish to inform you that the next meeting of the Pershore-Stamford Debating Society will be held in the Parish Rooms on Thursday November 26th, at 7.45 p.m.

Miss Rosemary Cathcart will open the meeting supporting the motion 'That this Society views with alarm the increasing folly of nations'. The opposer is Mr Keith Learoyd. The subject will be opened for debate when the speakers have concluded.

Yours faithfully
Stanley Archer

Letter asking for a club fixture

123 Adelaide Road
Chatsworth
Gloucester
CH5 2RG
16 July 19—

The Secretary
The United Rangers F.C.
Station Road
Cheltenham
CH2 9YR

Dear Sir

We are currently drawing up our fixture list for the coming season and are anxious to meet the United Rangers.

We usually play two elevens every Saturday, one at home and the other away.

The dates which we still have vacant are:

....

....

....

....

If any of these dates are convenient to your club, we shall be pleased to book them for both your first and second elevens. We do not mind which team plays on your ground and which on ours.

Hoping that we shall be able to meet,

Yours sincerely
A.S. Potter
(Secretary, Chatsworth Rovers)

Reply to a club asking for a fixture

Under the Elms
Porsham
Gloucester
G15 2RX
30 July 19—

Dear Mr Potter

In reply to your request for a fixture with our club, I wish to say that we shall be pleased to play you on Saturday January 30th; kick-off will be at 2.15 p.m.

We have booked your first eleven to play on our grounds at King George V Playing Fields in Porsham and for our second eleven to visit your ground. I hope these arrangements are suitable for you.

Yours sincerely
F. Halsey
(Secretary, The United Rangers F.C.)

Those who have had experience with the arranging of club fixtures know that many unnecessary letters have to be written because secretaries fail to supply adequate particulars. The date, the time, which eleven will be visiting and the location of the ground, if difficult to find, should all be given.

Letter announcing the annual meeting of a society

16, Blackford Road
Glasgow
G7 2RY
8 July 19—

Miss E. Ward
19 Bearsden Avenue
Glasgow
G15 9MN

Dear Madam

I wish to inform you that the annual meeting of the Blackford Debating Society will be held on July 30th at Central Hall, Blackford Road, starting at 8 p.m.

Motions must be submitted in writing to me by July 1st, if they are to be printed on the agenda.

The committee hope that it will be convenient for you to attend.

Yours faithfully
Agnes Hirchfield

Letter submitting a motion for an agenda

39 Atlantic Row
Newford
NE3 2DS
19 August 19—

R. Temple Esq.
53 Coverley Drive
Newford
NE6 1XP

Dear Sir

I have today received your letter, advising me that the next meeting of the Newford Debating Society is to be held on September 1st.

I would like to submit the following motion, for inclusion on the agenda:

'That in future, members who are in arrears with their subscriptions shall be denied the right of voting on matters affecting the policy of this society.'

Yours faithfully
F.K. Chesterfield

· 8 ·

ILLNESS AND DEATH

Writing a letter of sympathy is not an easy task. It is preferable to keep any such letters short and make sure that the tone is supportive and appropriate to your relationship with the person concerned.

Letter of sympathy and offer of help in a case of illness

54 Bowden Lane
Charlton
SE7 9DU
8 February 19—

Dear Jane

We are extremely sorry to hear that Ian is very ill, and we do hope that you will soon have some better news to report.

Is there any way in which we can help? At times like this, it is often hard to manage, so if there is anything we can do, please do not hesitate to let us know.

Would you like Tom to come here for a few days, as he is so young and must be taking up a great deal of your time? He would be quite happy with James and we should be delighted to have him.

With every sympathy,

Yours sincerely
Margaret and Philip

Letter of sympathy regarding someone who is ill (1)

39 Fircroft Road
Blackheath
SE3 5TH
26 January 19—

Dear Mr Gregory

I am extremely sorry to hear of your wife's illness, and I do hope that she will soon be much better.

It must be an anxious time for you and you have my fullest sympathy.

Let us hope that, in a short while, you will have some better news.

With kind regards,

Yours sincerely
Edgar Billing

Do not use this letter if it is known that the invalid is not likely to recover.

Letter of sympathy regarding someone who is ill (2)

39 Fircroft Road
Blackheath
SE3 5TH
26 January 19—

Dear Mr Gregory

I have heard that your wife is very ill and I am writing to say how sorry I am.

You must be dreadfully worried, but perhaps you will be able to gain some consolation from the knowledge that many of your friends are feeling for you.

My wife joins with me in sympathy.

Yours sincerely
Edgar Billing

Suitable in extreme cases when the invalid is not likely to recover.

Letter to an invalid

39 Fircroft Road
Blackheath
SE3 5TH
26 January 19—

Dear Mrs Gregory

We are extremely sorry to hear you are ill and we do hope and trust you will soon be better.

We are thinking of you every day and wondering how you are.

If there is anything we can do, please do not hesitate to make use of us. We shall phone, from time to time, to see how you are progressing.

With kindest regards,

Yours sincerely
Ada Billing

Letter written on behalf of a sick person

Lewington Grange
Lewington
Cheshire
LG4 5RY
5 December 19—

Dear Mrs Axford

It is very good of you to write such a cheery letter to Mother and the flowers you sent delighted her.

I am sorry to say she is still very ill. The nurse comes every day, and sometimes she has been twice. I am afraid it is going to be a long and weary business.

The only bright feature is Mother's courage. She is threatening to be out of bed within a week, which is, of course, an impossibility.

When she is a little better, she would enjoy a visit from you; but at present she is really too weak to see anybody.

Yours sincerely
Flora Perry

Letter to a friend in hospital

Avondale
Hampstead Drive
NW2 1JW
15 September 19—

Dear Arnold

I was so surprised to hear yesterday that you were in hospital, and have had to have an operation. I'm sorry that fate has been so unkind to you and I hope that it will not be long before you are back at home.

I don't know much about hospitals, but if anyone can find them amusing, I am sure you would be just the one to do so. You have always had the knack of seeing the funny side of a situation, and I guess you'll do it this time.

If I may come in and see you some time, it would be a pleasure to do so.

Best of luck,

Yours ever
Derek

Letter of thanks from an invalid

Ward 3
The Cottage Hospital
Dunham
DN9 8XQ
3 May 19—

Dear Mrs Fletcher

Now that I am able to sit up a little, I should like to thank you for the lovely flowers you sent in the other day. They are still as cheerful and fresh as ever.

It was good of you to think of me and I appreciate your kindness.

Fortunately, I am improving, but it is going to be a long haul. Still, I must not grumble, as the change is in the right direction.

Yours sincerely
Julia Troutbeck

Letter to a neighbour about an invalid

Croftholme
Taplow
TA3 2DR
8 May 19—

Dear Mrs Jones

I should be most grateful if you would ask your children to keep as quiet as possible for the next few days, as my husband is very ill. I know it is hard for them, but he needs as much sleep as possible for his recovery.

Thanking you in anticipation, and with good wishes,

Yours sincerely
Anne Marsh

Letter to a neighbour who is ill

19 Trehurst Crescent
Buxton
BN5 9NU
6 November 19—

Dear Mrs Mackay

I have only just heard that you are laid up and under the care of the doctor. I am so sorry I do not know you very well, but I should be very pleased to help you in any way I can.

Would you like me to come in and sit with you one afternoon? It would relieve your husband and be a change for you. I might then find out other ways in which I could be useful to you while you are ill.

Hoping you will soon recover,

Yours sincerely
Martha Brown

This sort of letter would usually be delivered by hand.

Letter in reply to the previous example

17 Trehurst Crescent
Buxton
BN5 9NV
7 November 19—

Dear Mrs Brown

It is so very kind of you to suggest coming in to sit with me. I shall be very pleased to see you if you would like to come tomorrow about 3 o'clock. I am afraid it is my fault that we have not been better acquainted, but I do not easily make friends.

I hope you will excuse a rather scribbled note, but I am confined to bed.

Looking forward to seeing you,

Yours sincerely
Agnes Mackay

Letter of condolence on a death

39 Fircroft Road
Blackheath
SE3 2BR
8 February 19—

Dear Mr Gregory

I have just heard of the sad death of your wife and Margaret and I would like to say how deeply sorry we are.

I cannot tell you how much I feel for you but I know you will realise that it has come to us as a great shock.

We both had a great admiration for Mrs Gregory and we hope you will find some slight consolation in the knowledge that we are grieving at her loss.

In deepest sympathy,

Yours sincerely
Edgar Billing

Letter informing a friend or relative of a death

69 Fursewood Gardens
Lincoln
LN1 9FD
10 May 19—

Dear Aunt Laura

I am sure you will be very sorry to hear that Mother died last night. The end was peaceful.

I shall write to you again later, when we have made the arrangements for the funeral.

Yours with love
Katherine

As the occasion is one when many people will have to be informed, the letter may be very brief and to the point.

Letter responding to the news of a death

798 Drury Lane
Lincoln
LN3 5MY
11 May 19—

Dearest Katherine

I am most distressed to hear of your mother's death and do hope you are coping in the sad circumstances.

It must be a great comfort to you to be able to feel that you were always so close to your mother. You certainly need not reproach yourself for anything.

I intend coming over to see you on Sunday (May 16th).

I am so sorry, dear.

Yours with love
Aunt Laura

Letter excusing absence from work after a relative's death

315 Hilltop Road
Hamberton
Shropshire
HB8 2DY
8 November 19—

F. Gilderson Esq.
3 The Market Square
Hamberton
HB2 5QS

Dear Sir

I am very sorry to say that my father died yesterday. In the circumstances, it will not be possible for me to come to the office for a few days.

I trust that you will excuse my absence and I apologise for the inconvenience I may cause.

Yours faithfully
Adela Cunningham

Letter notifying the time of a funeral

73 Westingford Street
NW8 2QN
8 January 19—

H. Young Esq.
3 Station Avenue
NW5 2LF

Dear Sir

I have been asked by Miss Yeoman to inform you that the funeral of her father will take place on Tuesday, January 11th, at Holy Trinity Church, Exford Street, NW8 4XP, at 1.30 p.m.

Yours faithfully
S. Gosling

Letter informing an executor of a death

3 Jedburgh Road
Richmond
Surrey
RD2 9LV
3 April 19—

Dear Mr Pinckney

I am sure you will be sorry to hear that my father died last night. He was in good health until about a week ago, when he suddenly became ill.

I see from his papers that he had appointed you as one of the executors of his will. I should be most grateful if you could contact me to discuss this matter as soon as is convenient to you.

Yours sincerely
Marjorie Ellam

This letter presumes that the writer is only slightly acquainted with the person to whom she is writing. Her main reason for sending the letter is to inform the executor of his duties.

———

Formal letter of thanks for sympathies following a death

69 Truscott Avenue
Burlington
Wolverhampton
W15 5XN
14 June 19—

Mr and Mrs Ackroyd and family
gratefully acknowledge your very kind expression of
sympathy in their sad loss and would like to thank you.

Such a letter is usually printed. It is sent to all who wrote or visited personally and also to those who sent wreaths.

· 9 ·

LANDLORD AND TENANT

This chapter concentrates on letters which will be useful in any matters relating to tenancy arrangements.

Letter from a landlord to a tenant, reminding him that the rent is due

6 High Street
Broadham
Sussex
BN9 5HE
28 December 19—

R. Cuthbert Esq.
2 Station Road
Brighton
BN3 4TP

Dear Sir

I have to remind you that the rent, due from you on December 25th, in respect of the premises situated at 54 Archway Street, has not yet been received.

I shall be obliged if you will send me a cheque in settlement at your earliest convenience.

Yours faithfully
John Stewart

Letter from a landlord to a tenant, requesting overdue rent

6 High Street
Broadham
Sussex
BN9 5HE
1 February 19—

R. Cuthbert Esq.
2 Station Road
Brighton
BN3 4TP

Dear Sir

I have to call your attention to the fact that the rent due from you for the quarter ending December 25th, in respect of the premises occupied by you at 54 Archway Street, has not yet been received.

I regret to have to inform you that unless a settlement is forthcoming without any further delay, I shall be compelled to take such steps as the law allows.

Yours faithfully
John Stewart

Letter from a landlord serving notice on a tenant

63 Woodhurst Drive
Poolford
Dorset
JO9 5TB
12 July 19—

Mr Peter Smith
94 Court Road
Poolford
Dorset
JO9 5TB

Dear Mr Smith

I have not received any rent form you since March 30 for the property which you rent at 94 Court Road. I am therefore forced to give you formal notice to leave. In accordance with your tenancy agreement with me, I am giving you four weeks' notice from the date of this letter.

Yours sincerely
Ian Graham

(Such a letter should be sent by recorded delivery.)

Letter to a landlord asking him to carry out repairs

60 Waldemar Avenue
NW16 4JE
29 June 19—

G.A. Blay Esq.
23 Highgrove Mansions
W3 4DX

Dear Sir

I regret to have to tell you that yesterday the high winds damaged a number of tiles on the property which I rent from you at the above address.

I should be glad if you could see that the matter is put right as soon as possible, since every time it rains water runs through one of the ceilings.

Yours faithfully
J. Sudbury

Letter to a landlord, as before, but affecting recurring repairs

60 Waldemar Gardens
NW16 4JE
29 June 19—

G.A. Blay Esq.
23 Highgrove Mansions
W3 4DX

Dear Sir

I am enclosing the rent of the above premises, for the quarter just ended.

I would like to draw your attention to the state of many of the rooms which are greatly in need of renovation. The sitting room and the front bedroom are both very bad.

I should be grateful if you could attend to this matter as soon as possible.

Yours faithfully
J. Sudbury

Letter from a landlord refusing to carry out repairs

43 Singleton Mews
SW14 3DL
19 January 19—

G. Hunter Esq.
27 Victoria Road
SW10 9XP

Dear Sir

I am in receipt of your letter of January 8th, and regret to have to inform you that it is impossible to consider any repairs to the house for some time to come.

During the last two years the major part of the rent has been absorbed by renovations and the property has been a severe drain on my own income. Therefore, while I do not wish to be unreasonable, I am unable to carry out any further repairs for the time being.

Yours faithfully
A. Gifford

Letter from a tenant asking for a reduction in rent

5 Antill Gardens
Brookhurst
Essex
BK12 9XV
28 January 19—

S. Ladberry Esq.
61 Turnfield Lane
Brookhurst
BK12 7VG

Dear Sir

I am writing to ask if you will agree to a reduction of the rent I am paying for the above address. I have lived here more than two years and, during that time have not asked for an excessive amount of repairs, having done many small jobs myself.

I now find that I am paying more for this house than the sums paid by many of my neighbours whose houses are regularly maintained by their landlord.

I should be grateful if you would consider my request and let me have a reply as soon as possible.

Yours faithfully
S.A. Maidman

_____

Letter from a landlord refusing to reduce the rent

61 Turnfield Lane
Brookhurst
Essex
BK12 7VG
12 February 19—

S.A. Maidman
5 Antill Gardens
Brookhurst
BK12 9XV

Dear Sir

I am sorry to say it is impossible to reduce the rent of the house of which you are the tenant.

When I originally fixed the rent I took into consideration that you were likely to be a good tenant, and put it at a low figure.

Were I to make a reduction, there would be very little left after paying for repairs and paying the ground rent. I was in fact wondering last quarter whether I ought not to raise the rent, owing to my increased outgoings.

With regrets,

Yours faithfully
S. Ladberry

Letter from a tenant threatening to leave if the rent is not reduced

5 Antill Gardens
Brookhurst
Essex
BK12 9XV
16 February 19—

S. Ladberry Esq.
61 Turnfield Lane
Brookhurst
BK12 7VG

Dear Sir

I am in receipt of your letter of 12th February in which you refuse to reduce the rent of this house.

I am sorry to say that, if this is your final decision, I shall be forced to seek accommodation elsewhere.

My wages have increased very little in the last ... years and I find there are houses nearby that suit my needs at lower rentals than yours.

In these circumstances, I must ask you to reconsider your decision, or I must move.

Yours faithfully
S.A. Maidman

Letter from a landlord raising the rent

61 Turnfield Lane
Brookhurst
Essex
BK12 7VG
3 March 19—

G. Lauriman Esq.
3 Denefield Cottages
Brookhurst
BK14 6HY

Dear Sir

I am sending you formal notice that, as from June 25th, 19—,
your rent will be increased from £ ... to £ ... per annum.

I am forced to take this step owing to the increase in the cost
of maintenance.

Yours faithfully
S. Ladberry

*Notices of this kind should be sent by registered mail and the receipt
kept, in order to avoid any dispute as to delivery. The landlord should
make sure that he gives the proper amount of notice if an agreement
exists.*

Letter from a landlord to an outgoing tenant

6 High Street
Broadham
Sussex
BN3 2JK
1 February 19—

S. Davies Esq.
3 The Terrace
Broadham
BN1 6NL

Dear Sir

As your tenancy expires at the end of this quarter, may I ask if you could allow a prospective tenant to look over the house?

Naturally, the person in question would only come by appointment and at a time entirely convenient to Mrs Davies and yourself.

I should be most grateful if you could assist me in this matter.

Yours faithfully
John Stewart

Letter from a tenant about overdue rent

3 Seacome Villas
Archery Fields
Arden
AN3 5FB
7 February 19—

M. Shawcross Esq.
10 Alexander Road
Arden
AN10 2TP

Dear Sir

I regret that you have had to write in connection with the rent, which is now overdue.

I am sorry to say that at the moment I am unable to pay the arrears. The last few months have proved a great strain on my finances, largely because ....

....

....

....

....

In all the circumstances, I would ask you to let the matter stand for a little while and, in the meantime, I will do my best to get the money together.

Yours faithfully
Peter A. Smithson

Fill in particulars, in the space left open, according to your personal conditions.

Letter to the environmental health department

25 Moreton Street
Angleford
AF10 6DU
12 May 19—

The Environmental Health Officer
Angleford Town Hall
Angleford
AF1 9BW

Dear Sir

I am the tenant at the above address and, for some considerable time have been uneasy about the sanitary conditions here. In particular, I find ....

....

....

....

....

I have written several times to the landlord concerning these matters and he refuses to take any notice.

In the circumstances, I am writing to inform you of what I believe are the conditions, in order that you may look into the matter.

Yours faithfully
Arthur Westlake

Before a tenant reports such a matter to the authorities he should make sure that his tenancy agreement throws the liability on the landlord and not on himself.

Letter asking for early release from a tenancy agreement

308 Cumberland Road
NW25 4XP
21 January 19—

C. Potter Esq.
24 Victoria Mansions
NW10 9DU

Dear Sir

My husband has just accepted the management of some large works near to Bristol and we are anxious to move into that neighbourhood as soon as possible. However, our lease of this house has still nine months to run. I should be grateful if you would let us know at your earliest convenience at what date, and on what terms, you would be prepared to release us from the remainder of our tenancy? We want, if possible, to get away by May 1st, and will, of course, be ready to meet any reasonable terms you are kind enough to offer us.

Regretting very sincerely that we find it necessary to make this move, and with our kind regards,

Yours faithfully
Mary Brookfield (Mrs)

Letter from a landlord to his letting agent

58 Wexford Avenue
Beckenham
Kent
BK3 9EO
4 July 19—

C. Rose
The Parade
Beckenham
Kent
BK3 4XL

Dear Sir

I acknowledge receipt of the statement of rents for my houses at nos 2 and 5 Starwick Road, for the month of June 19—. I am glad to see that the tenants are paying regularly.

I note, however, that repairs are again required to the small bathroom at no 2. This is the third occasion in four months that such repairs have been necessary. I should therefore ask you to ascertain whether this is due to careless usage on the part of the tenants, or whether work done by the plumber you engaged is faulty in some way.

I should be grateful if this matter could be attended to as quickly as possible, as I do not want any further repairs to be carried out on this bathroom until the cause of the problem is established.

Yours faithfully
G. Talbot

Letter to a housing advice centre about unfair eviction

Flat 2
Holmedale Court
College Road
Blessop
Lancs
UP8 4TC
29 August 19—

The Blessop Housing Advice Centre
Orion Precinct
Blessop
Lancs
UP8 6TG

Dear Sirs

I would be grateful if you could tell me if it is legal for a landlord to evict me despite the fact that I pay the rent regularly.

I have been renting a partly-furnished two-bedroomed flat at the above address for just over five years, during which time I have only once been in arrears with the rent. For the past year, the rent has been £115 per week and I have paid this sum to my landlord in person each week.

On 16th August, my landlord told me that he needed my flat for his brother-in-law's use. He gave me notice to leave by 15th September. I have told him that I cannot find alternative accommodation and that I will not leave. Yesterday he came to say that the builders will be arriving on 6th September to redecorate the flat for the new occupant.

I cannot possibly find another suitable flat at such short notice and would therefore much appreciate your advice as to my legal position.

Yours faithfully
Stuart Hall

· 10 ·

MONEY AND HOME

Financial arrangements relating to the home are the focus
of the sample letters in this chapter.

Letter querying a household account

84 Brownlows Gardens
Easterly
EY3 4TJ
4 January 19—

The General & District Gas Co.
23 High Street
Easterly
EY1 4ND

Dear Sirs

On receiving your account for the quarter's supply of gas, I
was astonished to find that the bill was for so large an amount.

As the consumption indicated is far greater than any previous
quarter and as there is no reason for supposing that we have
used more gas, I can only conclude that the meter is out of
order. Will you please be good enough to give the matter
your earliest attention?

Yours faithfully
S. McDonald

Letter asking for an estimate

29 Churchill Drive
Rotherton
RH19 6BD
19 July 19—

Alldays & Brown Ltd
Baldwin Street
Maidsgrove
Kent
RH9 6EU

Dear Sirs

We are considering having certain repairs done to the above premises. Roughly speaking, the work consists of

(1) ....

(2) ....

(3) ....

If you would like to offer an estimate, we shall be glad to give one of your men an opportunity of looking over the premises any day next week (except Saturday), between 10 a.m. and 5 p.m. Please telephone me on 0118 123 4567 so that we may arrange a convenient time.

Yours faithfully
Derwent Morgan

Letter accepting an estimate

28 Barnfield Close
Brackley
Lancs
LN3 8NM
7 October 19—

Your ref: SW 63/GW

Messrs Stokely and Wicks (Builders) Ltd
46 Winlow Lane
Brackley
Lancs
LN3 1ST

Dear Sirs

This letter is to confirm our acceptance of your estimate dated 4th October 19— for building repairs at the above address.

We also confirm that a start date of 3rd November is satisfactory.

We look forward to seeing you at 9 a.m. on that date.

Yours faithfully
George Wills

Letter asking a friend for a loan

7 Priory Grove
Nightingale Lane
Palmer's Green
N15 2SV
8 June 19—

My dear Hugh

I am extremely sorry to worry you on such a subject, but recent repairs to the house have exhausted my savings and I am finding myself in financial difficulties at the moment. If you could possibly let me have £500 or so for three or four months, it would see me safely round the corner and relieve my mind of a great strain. I have tried my brother William but, with his large family, he has no money to spare and cannot help me just now.

Don't hesitate to say 'no' if you really cannot do it – I am sure you will if you can.

Yours sincerely
Jack Thompson

Letter replying to a request for a loan (1)

309 The Broadway
Golder's Green
NW11 2VU
15 June 19—

My dear Jack

What rough luck! I'm extremely sorry for you and your wife. As it happens, I can easily do what you ask and enclose a cheque for £500. Don't feel obliged to pay it back in three or four months, although I shall appreciate having it by the end of the year.

My kind regards to both of you,

Yours ever
Hugh Woodward

Letter replying to a request for a loan (2)

309 The Broadway
Golder's Green
NW11 2VU
10 June 19—

My dear Jack

I was extremely sorry to hear your bad news. Unfortunately, I cannot help you in the way you suggest. I am, however, sending £100, which is all I can do for you at the moment. I hope it will clear you of your most pressing difficulties and give you time to try some other friend. Drop me a line if you fail elsewhere and I will, if possible, let you have another £50 when I get my salary cheque at the end of the month.

No hurry for repayment and don't let your wife worry at all.

All good wishes,

Yours ever
Hugh Woodward

Letter requesting repayment of a loan (1)

39 Grove Drive
Leicester
LE13 5DL
8 August 19—

Dear Mr Angus

Two or three months ago you were suffering financial difficulties and, at some inconvenience to myself, I lent you £100.

Now, it happens that I need the money which I handed over to you. Will you therefore, please let me have the return of this sum?

Yours sincerely
S. Gurry

Letter requesting repayment of a loan (2)

39 Grove Drive
Leicester
LE13 5DL
8 September 19—

Dear Mr Angus

A month has passed since I wrote to you asking for the return of the £100 which I lent you two or three months previously.

As you have not bothered to reply, I take it that you only intend doing so under compulsion. I am, therefore, informing you that, unless the debt is paid before the end of the week, I shall put your letter and the receipt before my solicitor.

Yours truly
S. Gurry

Letter to solicitors about the sale of a house

32 Church Gardens
Dunham
Bucks
15 May 19—

Upley, Pope and Dykes, Solicitors
5–7 Broad Street
Dunham
Bucks
SB3 1BN

Dear Sirs

Re: 32 Church Gardens, Dunham, Bucks

This is to confirm our conversation of 14th May with Mrs Williams of your office, in which we agreed to your partnership handling the conveyancing arrangements for both the sale of 32 Church Gardens and the purchase of New Farm, Chilton Maltravers, Bucks.

I understand that your estimated fee is £950.00 plus VAT, stamp duty, land registration and search and mortgage costs.

The purchasers of 32 Church Gardens are:
> Mr and Mrs S. Boyer
> 16 Berry Close
> Dunham
> Bucks
> SB8 5SN

The vendors of New Farm are Mr and Mrs R. Chapman.

Please let me know what further information you require as to mortgage account numbers, deeds, etc.

Yours faithfully
Robin Austin

Letter to estate agents about the sale of a house

32 Church Gardens
Dunham
Bucks
15 May 19—

Robinson Whitlow, Estate Agents
19–21 High Street
Dunham
Bucks
SB6 1BD

For the attention of Miss Wicks

Dear Miss Wicks

Re: 32 Church Gardens, Dunham, Bucks

This is to confirm our agreement that your company will act as sole agents for the sale of the above property at a commission rate of 2% plus VAT. We understand that should we at any time decide to offer the house for sale through a joint agency, then the commission rate due to your company will be 3% plus VAT.

We also wish to confirm the sales particulars you have supplied are satisfactory.

Yours sincerely
Robin Austin

Letter to purchasers about the sale of a house

32 Church Gardens
Dunham
Bucks
19 May 19—

Mr and Mrs S. Boyer
16 Berry Close
Dunham
Bucks
SB8 5SN

Dear Mr and Mrs Boyer

Re: 32 Church Gardens

I understand from our solicitors that all the arrangements for the sale of the above property, and also for our purchase of New Farm, are proceeding satisfactorily. We expect exchange of contracts to take place at the beginning of August and completion at the end of the third week of August.

As agreed, I am listing here the items that we are selling as fixtures and fittings, but which do not form part of the main contract:

Brass door handles throughout
Carpets and underlays in all downstairs rooms and hall, landing and stairs

Slatted blinds on lounge patio doors
Lounge wall lights
Roller blinds in kitchen and bathroom
Bathroom wall cabinet
Curtains in master bedroom

Total Price **£550.00**

Please send a cheque for this sum, made payable to R and J
Austin, to our solicitors prior to the completion date.

Yours sincerely
Robin Austin

To an insurance company about a burglary

29 Revell Road
Birmingham
B4 8BB
21 May 19—

Reliant Insurance Company Ltd
Pimlico Street
London
SW1 8GH

Dear Sirs

Re: Policy Number LN 985968

I wish to inform you that my home, at the above address, was
burgled on the night of 19th May 19—.

Although my wife and I were in the house all evening, the
theft was not discovered until 7.30 on the morning of 20th
May when I realised that the kitchen window was open. We
then noticed that several items were missing and telephoned
the police who are now handling an investigation.

I should be pleased if you would send me a claim form so that
I may give you a full list of the missing items, with their

replacement values. I shall be happy to give you any further information you may need in order to make a settlement without delay.

Yours faithfully
Barry Spinks

Letter to a finance company about difficulty with repayments

15 Dower Road
Worthing
Sussex
WT2 9NP
1 July 19—

Southern Leasing
12-14 Arlington Square
London
SW1 6HL

Dear Sirs

Re: Agreement 91837/SDF/986

I am having some difficulty in meeting the repayments for the car which I bought last year under the terms of the above agreement. To date, I have paid regularly every month, but I now find that my outgoings are more than I can afford.

I do not wish to default on my debt to your company and would therefore be most grateful if you would consider allowing me to make smaller payments over a longer period.

Please could you let me know if such a change to my existing arrangement is possible and, if so, what terms you are able to offer me.

Yours faithfully
Peter Mackieson

Letter to building society about difficulty with mortgage repayments

5 Green Lane
Abingdon
Oxon
AB3 5UN
11 July 19—

The Manager
Midlands Building Society
Upper High Road
Closter
Oxon
LM8 9AB

Dear Sir

Re: Mortgage Policy Number 098/LBJ/85

I am writing to inform you that I am having difficulty in meeting my mortgage repayments.

My employers for the last 15 years, J.M. Smith and Company, went into liquidation in January and I was made redundant. I am actively seeking another position but, as you will appreciate, employment is not easy to find in this area at present.

I have some savings in addition to my redundancy payment, but I am finding it hard to meet all my commitments. I therefore wonder if it might be possible for me to reduce my monthly payments by 20% and extend the term of the mortgage to allow for this?

I hope that you will give sympathetic consideration to my situation and agree to the temporary measures I have suggested.

I would of course be pleased to come and discuss this matter further with you if you feel it would be helpful.

Yours faithfully
Malcolm James

Letter to a bank about the loss of a cheque card

51 Church Street
Royburn
RO3 9XD
11 May 19—

E.R. Cox
The Manager
London and District Bank
Amberley Drive
Royburn
Berkshire
RO1 2PK

Dear Mr Cox

Re: Account Number 0347599 S. F. Dennis

I write to confirm my telephone conversation to your office this morning, in which I explained that I have lost my cheque card, number 3798798.

I first noticed the loss yesterday evening. I last used the card on 8th May when I cashed a cheque, number 48569060, at your High Street branch in Royburn.

Yours sincerely
Simon Dennis

Letter to a bank manager asking him to stop payment of a cheque

51 Church Street
Royburn
RO3 9XD
8 July 19—

E.R. Cox Esq.
London and District Bank
Amberley Drive
Royburn
RO1 2PK

Dear Sir

Will you please stop payment of cheque 42480006 dated July 6th. It was signed by me in favour of E. Taylor, for the sum of £50.

Yours faithfully
S. Dennis

A cheque should only be stopped when there is some very good reason for doing so, such as its loss by the recipient or fraud.

Letter to a bank about an overdrawn account

30 Eton Street
Hungerford
Berkshire
HG8 0EW
4 August 19—

E. R. Cox
The Manager
London and District Bank
Amberley Drive
Royburn
Berkshire
RO1 2PK

Dear Sir

Re: Account Number 70790856, S. Black

It will have come to your attention that my account has been marginally overdrawn on four occasions in the last two months. As I have bills for repairs to my car due to be paid soon, I am afraid that this will happen again and so I would be grateful if you could arrange for me to have proper overdraft facilities up to £500. I would expect to need this until the end of July next year when my salary is due to increase and I shall be able to repay the debt.

I would of course be happy to come in and discuss the matter with you if you think that this is necessary.

Yours faithfully
Sylvia Black

Letter to an insurance company about the death of a policyholder

25 St. Andrews Court
Maidstone
Kent
MN6 9HD
15 July 19—

Trust Insurance Co. Ltd
69 Croft Land
London
EC1 6DR

Dear Sirs

Re: Trust Insurance Policy Number 9469086

The holder of the above policy, Gerald Young, died on 28th June. I enclose a copy of the death certificate.

I am executor of his will. I should be grateful if you could inform me as to the amount of money the beneficiary will receive and on what date. Also confirmation is required that the deceased's widow, Mrs Gloria Mary Young, is still the named beneficiary.

If you require further information or documents, please let me know.

Yours faithfully
Andrew Blake
Encs.

Letter about a refusal of credit facilities

20 Cedar Road
Hemel Hempstead
HH7 9BX
18 December 19—

The Manager
Maybrick Stores
678 Pinder Street
London
W2A 4NM

Dear Sir

I am writing to ask why I have been refused credit by your company.

I came to your shop on 18th January to buy a washing machine and tumble drier, at a total cost of £697. I understood from leaflets displayed in your store, and from advertisements in local newspapers, that you offer credit facilities to your customers and I therefore asked for the necessary paperwork to be prepared. I was most shocked when I was told that this would not be possible in my case, a decision confirmed by the department manager, Mr Smith.

I should appreciate your explanation for this refusal which has caused me considerable inconvenience and embarrassment.

Yours faithfully
Andrew Blackstock

Letter to a credit reference agency about a personal file

20 Cedar Road
Hemel Hempstead
HH7 9BX
18 January 19—

Black and Company
Credit House
Comley
Berks
RG8 6SG

Dear Sirs

I understand from Mr A. Mathew, manager of Maybrick Stores, Pinder Street, London, that you are holding a file relating to my credit status. Since I have recently been refused credit by Maybrick Stores, I assume that the information you have about me, which you supplied to them, is unfavourable.

I would be grateful if you would send me a copy of your file on my financial affairs; I enclose a cheque for £ ... which I understand is the amount of your handling charges.

Yours faithfully
Andrew Blackstock

Letter to a company about a lost document

54 Amberley Road
Appleton
Essex
AN3 4DV
31 January 19—

The Secretary
The Premier Tailors Ltd
Broadway
Appleton
AN1 9XR

Dear Sir

Recently, you sent me a dividend warrant for £20, in respect of 200 shares which I hold in your company.

Unfortunately the warrant has been destroyed or mislaid. In the circumstances, would you inform me whether it is possible to issue a duplicate or, if this cannot be done, what course you adopt in such cases.

Yours faithfully
K. Brightwell

· 11 ·

BIRTHS AND
BIRTHDAYS

Births and birthdays are often occasions for very personal
and informal notes, cards or letters. These sample
letters will help you if you are not sure of the form of
words needed on particular occasions.

Letter announcing a birth

56 Glendower Court
Gloucester
GL9 5EU
3 June 19—

Dear Miss Fulford

I am pleased to tell you that I am sending the following
announcement to the *Daily Telegraph*.

Hillman: On 2nd June 19— at The Simpson Maternity
Hospital, Gloucester, to Geoffrey and Margery Hillman, a
son.

I am sure you will be pleased to hear that Margery and the
baby are both doing excellently.

Yours sincerely
Geoffrey Hillman

*On these occasions, it may be difficult for a husband to write suitable
letters informing people who are not close friends. A letter in the above
form gets over this in a neat manner.*

Reply to a birth announcement

64 Cedarwood Terrace
Westbourne Grove
W2 5PR
8 June 19—

Dear Mr Hillman

I was delighted to learn from your letter that you and Margery have a son. You must both feel very proud.

Please give my love to Margery and tell her I am so glad she is feeling well. I should love to come and see her when I may.

It was extremely kind of you to let me know, especially as you must be finding life rather busy at the moment.

Yours sincerely
Barbara Fulford

Letter of congratulation to a lady on the birth of a grandchild

Tessington Manor House
Shropshire
GU3 2RS
5 March 19—

My dear Mrs Gillingham-Lake

Do accept my congratulations on becoming a grand-mother. I was so pleased to hear that dear Julia had started off with a son and I am told that he is a very bonny boy! How proud you must be! I am dying for the time to come when I may go and see Julia and her son. Have they decided on a name yet? I am so glad to know that Julia has Angela Billing for a nanny. I believe she is excellent.

I hope you are quite fit, and that the family is in the best of health.

Yours sincerely
Lily Holmes-Rogers

Letter to a relative on his birthday

73 Marchmont Drive
Cambuslang
Glasgow
G15 9XP
18 February 19—

Dear Uncle Bob

It is your birthday tomorrow, and I am scribbling a note to send you my best wishes on the occasion.

I am afraid I don't know much about the things that uncles like for presents, so, to be on the safe side, I am sending you some of your usual brand of Scotch. I hope you like it as much as I like the present you sent for my birthday.

Give my love to Aunt Mary.

Your affectionate nephew
David

Letter of thanks for a birthday present

763 Archerhill Street
Glasgow
G3 4EB
20 February 19—

Dear David

It was very nice of you to remember my birthday and even nicer to spend your pocket money on buying me some whisky. You will be amused to hear that there was not a single drop in the house when yours arrived it came at exactly the right moment.

Tell Mother that it is so long since she came to see us that we are beginning to wonder if she has forgotten us.

Why not bring her over next Sunday?

All the best
Uncle Bob

Letter expressing thanks for a birthday present

803 Coalville Road
Edgbaston
Birmingham
B3 9DN
19 January 19—

My dear Margery

How sweet of you to think of me on my birthday. Your pretty and useful gift is very welcome, but what I appreciate most are your thoughtful wishes. It is nice of you to write and not forget me.

Give my love to your mother.

Your affectionate aunt
Elizabeth

Letter accompanying a twenty-first birthday present

The Limes
Kingswood Avenue
Chesterton
Surrey
CH9 3PT
31 March 19—

Dear Vivienne

I want to send you my congratulations on your Coming of Age next Friday. I hope it will be a very happy and memorable day for you.

I enclose a small gift which I hope you will like.

Yours sincerely
Aunt Dorothy

Letter of thanks for a twenty-first birthday present

Queen's Drive
Chesterton
Surrey
CH8 4DW
3 April 19—

Dear Aunt Dorothy

Thank you so much for your present. It is really lovely.

I had such a wonderful time yesterday that now I feel exhausted. Everybody was so good to me that I was quite overwhelmed.

When are you coming to see me again?

Yours sincerely
Vivienne

· 12 ·

DOMESTIC MATTERS

L etters in this chapter deal with a range of circumstances to do with the home and family.

Letter explaining a daughter's absence from work

37 Brierfield Road
Mitcham
MM9 3RB
5 June 19—

W. Griffiths Esq.
Messrs Pears, Wayward & Hope

Dear Sir

I am sorry to report that my daughter Elizabeth will be unable to come to the office on Monday, as she had a bad fall yesterday.

The doctor says her injuries are not serious, but he recommends 48 hours' rest.

She very much regrets the inconvenience she is causing you and hopes you will excuse her.

Yours faithfully
Henry Jones

Letter explaining absence from work (1)

754 Grovers Lane
Beckenham
Kent
BN3 9BF
3 February 19—

F. Grainger Esq.
The London Sheet Metal Co. Ltd
Shawford
BN15 2LZ

Dear Sir

I am sorry I was unable to attend work today; my wife's illness has taken a more serious turn and I had to remain at home with her.

I hope to arrange matters so that I shall be able to come to work as usual tomorrow, or the next day at the latest. If circumstances change, however, I will inform you immediately.

Yours faithfully
Edwin Mander

Letter explaining absence from work (2)

Hill Top
Burwash
Hythe
3 February 19—

E. Angus Esq.
Brown & Son Ltd
High Street
Burwash
BR2 9JW

Dear Sir

I much regret that I have not been able to come into the office this week. As my wife explained over the phone. I am suffering from an attack of flu and am unable to get out of bed. I have been visited by the doctor and, in his opinion, I shall not be fit to return until next Monday.

I am exceedingly sorry to have caused you inconvenience, but it has been absolutely unavoidable.

Yours faithfully
J. Simpson

In letters of this kind, give some idea of the nature of the illness but do not go into minute detail.

Letter to a newsagent cancelling daily papers

54 The Chase
Kingsford
Essex
KG4 3BY
2 August 19—

S. Boydell Esq.
High Street
Kingshord
KG2 8NJ

Dear Sir

As we shall be away on holiday for a short time from August 4th, will you please stop the delivery of all papers.

We shall require the papers on August 4th.

Yours faithfully
Arthur Reed

Note that the date must be made quite clear.

Letter to a local builder

48 Hunter's Lane
Harringay
N22 9WE
5 April 19—

A. Burroughs Esq.
Grange Road
Harringay
N22 4DE

Dear Sir

We have four or five sash lines that are broken and a door that needs repairing.

Could you send a man to have a look at these things? Please do not arrange for him to come on Monday before 12 noon, or on Tuesday after 3 p.m.

Yours faithfully
Ada Champion

Letter requesting a free sample

16 Halifax Street
Canterbury
Kent
CT6 8NM
19 November 19—

Castle Flooring Ltd
Dept DM 15
Queen Mary's Road
London
NW6 3KT

Dear Sirs

Please send me a free sample of your 'No Waste' floor covering. I enclose a stamped, self-addressed envelope.

Yours faithfully
N Chatterton
Encs.

You do not need to mention where you saw the advertisement. The firm will know from the reference code 'Dept DM 15' which in this case might mean the fifteenth advertisement they placed in the Daily Mail.

Letter ordering goods advertised for sale

634 Crescent Road
Ambleford
Hants.
AB2 9JT
18 July 19—

Messrs Berry and Berry Ltd
Bargain Dept.
High Street
Winchester
SO23 2YL

Dear Sirs

In today's *Daily Express* you advertise overalls at £5.50.

Please send me two sets, one blue and one green, both in 46 in. length.

I enclose my cheque for £12 to include the cost of postage.

Yours faithfully
Annie Turnbury (Mrs)

If the advertisement gives a serial numbering to the goods, be careful to quote it, as it will help to avoid mistakes.

Letter requesting servicing of a domestic appliance

17 Hillside Lane
Lincoln
LN3 9YG
21 September 19—

Lincoln Gas
4 Dover Street
Lincoln
LN4 6DG

Dear Sirs

I would like to have my central heating system serviced under the special 'parts only' plan which you advertised in the *Lincoln Post* this week. My system is a Drayton 600.

Please let me know the earliest date on which your engineer could call. An appointment after 2 p.m. on any day would be most convenient.

Yours faithfully
A. Barkworth

Letter complaining about environmental nuisance

17 Seaview Road
Brighton
BN1 7FD
19 February 19—

The Environmental Health Officer
Copley Borough Council
High Street
Copley
Sussex
BN3 4PP

Dear Sir

I wish to complain about the early start being made by builders working on the flats in Spelthorne Park Road, which is just a few metres from the back of our house.

For the last few days, work has commenced as early as 5 a.m. I am sure you will agree that such an early start cannot be permitted as it is impossible to sleep once work has begun.

I would be most grateful if you could look into this as soon as possible and inform me of what action you will be taking.

Yours faithfully
S.J. Carter

Letter of complaint to a neighbour

36 Seaview Lane
Ferryford
Sussex
FD5 2BG
8 July 19—

Dear Mr Henslowe

I am sorry to have to appear unneighbourly, but I must really ask you to do something about your dog. Recently it has been coming into my garden and doing a great deal of damage. It has ruined quite a number of plants and has also spoilt the appearance of the flower beds.

I am afraid that none of this would have happened had your fences been in good order.

I hope that you will see to it that I am put to no further trouble.

Yours sincerely
G. Ripon

Letter announcing a change of address

16 Station Road
Hartley
Ripon
RR5 3ER
16 May 19—

The Manager
Central Bank Ltd
4 Market Street
Hartley
Ripon
RR5 4BG

Dear Sir

Accounts: P. & J. Nayland, 12345670; J. Nayland, 98765434

Please note that from 29th May 19— our new address will be:

> 16 Willmore Gardens
> Hartley
> Ripon
> RR6 7TG   Telephone 01234 567890

Yours faithfully
Peter and Janet Nayland

Letter of objection to a planning application

38 Burfield Road
Brockford
Cheshire
C8 6FR
1 June 19—

The Chief Planning Officer
Brockford Council
Brockford Town Hall
218–240 Cross Road
Brockford
Cheshire
C8 6FR

Dear Sir

Re: Planning Application Number 179463

I wish to object to the above planning application.

Having viewed the plans, I am sure that this building, if constructed, would block off the light from my downstairs rooms and much of my back garden during the afternoon and evening.

I request that you take this into account when considering this application and suggest that you reject it forthwith.

Yours faithfully
R. Hancock (Ms)

Letter to a holiday agent seeking accommodation

68 Round Lane
Boundary Road
Heathfield
HA4 5DT
30 June 19—

Messrs Beadmore & Long
10 Friar Street
Barrowden
BD2 9XP

Dear Sirs

Having seen your advertisement in *Dalton's Weekly*, I am writing to ask if you have, on your books, a furnished house which is available for the months of August and September?

My requirements are:

- … bedrooms
- … reception rooms
- … bathrooms
- … distance from sea, at most
- … rent (inclusive).

I should be pleased to receive details of any houses which you consider may fit my requirements.

Yours faithfully
A.B. Mitchell (Mrs)

Letter accepting holiday apartments

62 Bassett Road
Willesden
NW10 2DY
5 July 19—

Dear Mrs Fitch

Thank you for your letter regarding accommodation for me and my family. I am writing to accept your terms of £ ... per week, which I understand includes all bills except the telephone.

In a few days I shall write telling you at what time on July 15th we shall arrive and I shall then include, as you have so kindly suggested, a list of the groceries we shall require at the start of the holiday.

We shall be leaving by midday on July 19th.

Yours sincerely
Rose Woodfield (Mrs)

Enquiry to a hotel in Europe

4 Southborne Road
Cookham
Berks
SL6 2RT
17 August 19—

The Manager
Hotel de la Poste
Villeblanc 1009
Brussels
Belgium

Dear Sir

Thank you for your kind hospitality during our stay at your hotel last week. We very much enjoyed our visit and hope to return some time next year.

Unfortunately, my wife has discovered that she left her brown walking shoes in Room 304 of the hotel. If they have been found, she would be very grateful to have them returned to her. We would, of course, reimburse you for the costs involved.

With our best wishes,

Yours faithfully
Alec Green

Letter of complaint to a tour operator

3 Orchard Mews
Nottingham
N2 9HF
30 August 19—

The Manager
Summer Tours Ltd
27 White Lane
Nottingham
N3 7XC

Dear Sir

Re: Holiday Ref. H056; Receipt No. A10578

I am writing to complain about the accommodation provided for my wife and me on the above holiday from 11th to 24th August 19—.

I booked the holiday at your offices on 16th February. At that time it was agreed that we would have an air-conditioned room with balcony and private bathroom. This was confirmed in writing by your Mr Jones on 20th February. However, when we arrived at the hotel on 11th August we were shown to a room which had none of these amenities. We immediately complained to your courier, Alan Smith, but were told that the hotel had made a mistake over the booking and no other room was available.

The standard of accommodation which we were forced to accept severely affected our enjoyment of the holiday. In light of this, and the fact that your company will have paid less for this room than the one advertised, I therefore expect an appropriate rebate on the sum paid.

I look forward to hearing from you and receiving your cheque in the very near future.

Yours faithfully
Robert Brown

GRAMMAR
APPENDIX

Correct grammar and spelling are essential if a piece of written work is to create a good impression. This section contains some rules and guidelines which may be helpful to anyone writing letters.

Punctuation

The chief punctuation marks are:

. full stop
, comma (placed on the line)
; semi-colon
: colon
? question mark
! exclamation mark
' apostrophe (placed above the line)
' ' quotation marks (placed above the line)

A full stop is used at the end of a sentence or after a word that is abbreviated. Any letter following a full stop at the end of a sentence must be a capital letter starting a new sentence.

Example: I went yesterday. Full stop at the end because the sentence is completed. *Jones and Co. is our company name.* Full stops at the end of the sentence and after Co. because it is an abbreviation.

The comma has very many uses, but its chief function is to divide up sentences into small portions, so that the meaning may be easier to understand. But it is very easy to get into the habit of using so many commas that one is placed after almost every word. Therefore, commas should be used only when necessary.

The function of a comma is evident in a sentence such as the following:

Charles Prince of England arrived in Paris. Without punctuation, the meaning of this sentence is ambiguous. Insert a comma after *Prince* and *England* – *Charles Prince, of England, arrived in Paris* – and the statement evidently refers to a gentleman whose name is Charles Prince.

Insert a comma after *Charles* and *England* – *Charles, Prince of England, arrived in Paris* – and the statement obviously refers to His Royal Highness.

Another use of the comma is when it replaces the word *and* or any similar conjunction, in order to avoid repetition: *The boy and the girl and the man went for a walk.* This is, of course, clumsy and the first 'and' should be omitted. Its place is taken by a comma – *The boy, the girl and the man went for a walk.*

Explanatory words or phrases, such as *however, nevertheless, in fact, consequently, therefore* and *indeed,* when they come in a sentence, require a comma both before and after them, unless they form the opening or closing word of the passage, when they need only one comma. The following examples will explain this use:

She said, in fact, that she would come. (*In fact,* two commas.)
In fact, she said she would come. (*In fact,* a comma after.)
She said she would come, in fact. (*In fact,* a comma before.)

Commas may also be used around phrases in a sentence. Let us start with a short sentence such as *The man gave the beggar 50p.* If we want to add to this sentence, the information that the man had a pocketful of change, the wording becomes *The man, having a pocketful of change, gave the beggar 50p.* We have added a phrase to the original sentence and, because a piece has been added, it needs a comma both before and after it.

The semicolon is used to separate two distinct passages which are put together to form one statement: *Money is useful;*

health is even more so. The pause provided by the semicolon adds more contrast and emphasis, than would be suggested by a comma.

The colon is used immediately before a list of things, as: *The following words are nouns: boy, cat, dog, fish, men.* It may also be used to link an introduction to a fuller explanation, as in *I wish to draw the following matters to your attention:.*

A question mark is needed at the end of a question and here it is necessary to distinguish between the end of the question and the end of the sentence, as the two may not be the same. Look at these three examples:

(a)   *Will you come to see me?*

(b)   *'Will you come to see me?' she asked.*

(c)   *'Will you come to see me,' she asked?*

(a) This is merely a sentence which entirely forms the question and, therefore, no doubt can arise as to where the question mark is to come.

(b) This question does not make up the whole of the sentence. Therefore, the question mark comes at the end of the question and not at the end of the sentence.

(c) This is incorrect because the question mark is at the end of the statement and so includes the question plus words that are not part of the question.

An exclamation mark follows a word or phrase expressing strong emotion, such as: *Alas! the worst happened,* or *Long may he reign!* It is, also, commonly used to indicate emphasis or exaggeration and sometimes even sarcasm: *You are too kind!* or *It is ridiculous!* It is unlikely to be used in any formal letter.

Note: When an exclamation or question mark is used, it replaces a full stop or comma. So an exclamation or question mark and a full stop (or comma) are never placed side by side.

An apostrophe is used to to indicate possession as in *the boy's book, the BBC's policy.* It is also used to show that something has been missed out, as in *I'll* (I shall) and *don't* (do not). These forms would not usually be written in a formal letter.

Note that *it's* stands for *it is* and so should not be used in the possessive form (*the cat washed its face*). Apostrophes should never be used before the 's' in plurals as in *the three cat's* – this is a bad mistake.

Quotation marks, often called inverted commas, are used at the beginning and end of words, phrases or sentences which are actually said or quoted. But do note that they must be the words actually used and not words very much like them. For instance, *He said, 'I do not think it will rain,'* is a repetition of the very words the person used; therefore, the quotation marks are required. But *He said that he did not think it would rain* does not repeat the actual words used, so the quotation marks are not required.

A dash is used to mark a break in the continuity of the reasoning. *Example: He brought the money – not that I asked for it.*

The hyphen, similar in form to the dash, though shorter, does the opposite function. While the dash causes a break, the hyphen joins simple words together to make compound words. *Examples: day-to-day, tug-of-war* and *love-in-a-mist*.

When to use capital letters

A capital letter should be used:

(1) At the beginning of every sentence.

(2) For the initial letter of every proper noun, such as a person's name, the name of a town, country, nation, etc.

(3) For the initial letter of every proper adjective; that is to say, adjectives made from proper nouns. *Examples:* The *English* people, the *Indian* mutiny, the *American* accent.

(4) Whenever the personal pronoun *I* is written, no matter where it is placed in a sentence.

(5) For the first letter of the days of the week *Sunday, Monday, Tuesday,* etc., months of the year *January, February, March,* etc. and religious festivals such as *Easter, Christmas, Ramadan, Passover,* etc.

(6) For the first letter of every line of poetry.

(7) For the first letter of the names of the Deity, as *God, Lord, Allah,* etc., and sometimes for the personal attributes of the Deity, or for pronouns used in place of the name, as *His, Who, Glory,* etc.

(8) For the first letter of a quotation put in quotation marks.

(9) For the first letter of a title, as *Queen Elizabeth, War of Independence, Daily Mail.* It is also advisable to use a capital for each important word in the title of a book or play, etc., as *It's Never Too Late to Mend.* This is preferable to *It's never too late to mend.*

(10) For the first letter of common nouns when they are personified, as *Come, sweet Charity.*

Rules for spelling

There are hundreds of rules regarding the spelling of words in the English language, and a complete list of them would probably not help the average person. It might even be confusing. Therefore, only the chief rules are given here.

Note: The consonants are *b,c,d,f,g,h,j,k,l,m,n,p,q,r,s,t, v,w,x,y,z.*

The vowels are *a,e,i,o,u.*

(1) When a word ends in *y* and has a consonant preceding the *y*, and you want to change the tense or add a syllable to the word, change the *y* into *i* and add the syllable in question.

Example: Carry becomes *carried*, not *carryed*.

This rule does not apply when the added syllable begins with *i*.

Example: Carry becomes *carrying*.

It does not apply when the addition is the possessive *'s*.

Example: Larry becomes *Larry's*.

Care must be taken to note that this rule only holds when the *y* is preceded by a consonant. If a vowel comes immediately before the *y*, there is usually no change. But there are certain exceptions, which are mostly words of one syllable. The following, therefore, should be noted:

Pay becomes *paid*.

Lay becomes *laid*.

Say becomes *said*.

Delay becomes *delayed*.

Essay becomes *essayed*.
Repay becomes *repaid*.

(2) When adding a syllable beginning with a vowel to a word that ends with an unsounded *e*, omit the *e* and add the extra syllable. For example:

Move becomes *movable*, not *moveable*.

If the word ends with *oe*, do not omit the *e*, but retain it and add the extra syllable. For example:

Shoe becomes *shoeing*, not *shoing*.

If the word ends with *ce* or *ge*, do not omit the *e* when *ous* or *able* are to be added. For example:

Notice becomes *noticeable*

Peace becomes *peaceable*

Courage becomes *courageous*.

If, by omitting the *e*, the meaning of the word may be ambiguous, the *e* should be retained. For example: *Singe* becomes *singeing* and not *singing*, as this would confuse with *singing* (vocal).

If a word ends with *ee* and the syllable that you wish to add begins with an *e*, one of the three *e's* must disappear. For example: *Agree* becomes *agreed*, not *agreeed*.

(3) The previous rule applies only when the added syllable commences with a vowel. If, however, the added syllable begins with a consonant, the final *e* is retained. For example: *Peace* becomes *peaceful*, not *peacful*.

There are certain exceptions, however. For example:

Awe becomes *awful*.

Argue becomes *argument*.

Due becomes *duly*.

True becomes *truly*.

Whole becomes *wholly*.

(4) Final consonants are not doubled, except *f, l* and *s*.

The following are exceptions to this rule: *add, burr, butt, buzz, ebb, egg, err, inn, odd, purr, rudd.*

(5) A one-syllable word ending in *f*, *l* or *s*, which is preceded by a vowel, doubles the last consonant. For example: *ball*, *cuff*, *puss*.

There are a good many exceptions to this rule such as *if*, *of*, *as*, *gas*, *his*, etc.

(6) Words of more than one syllable ending in *f*, *l* and *s*:

(a) Double the final *f*, as *distaff*.

(b) Usually double the final *s*, as *harass*.

(c) Do not double the final *l*, as *until*.

Exceptions are *atlas*, *alas*, *bias*, *Christmas*.

(7) *K* seldom comes at the end of a word of more than one syllable. For example, *critic*, *terrific*, *traffic*.

Exceptions are *attack*, *fetlock*, *forelock*, *paddock*, *ransack*.

(8) Words of one syllable ending in *k* usually have the *k* preceded by *c* after a single vowel, but have no *c* after diphthong or consonant. Thus:

Sack (short vowel).

Book (diphthong).

Bank (consonant).

Remember, however, *arc*, *disc*, *lac*, *zinc*.

(9) One-syllable words and words accented on the final syllable, which end with a single vowel and a consonant, double the last consonant when a suffix beginning with a vowel is added to them.

For example, if *ing* is to be added to the word *begin* which ends with a vowel and a consonant, the consonant *n* is doubled before the *ing* is added. In the same way:

Beg becomes *beggar*

Begin becomes *beginning*.

Glad becomes *gladden*.

Confer becomes *conferred*.

Rebel becomes *rebellion*.

In the words *confer* and *conferred*, the emphasis is on the *'fer'* and so rule 9 holds good. But in making the word *preference* form *prefer*, the emphasis is thrown forward on the *'pref'*. Rule 9 does not apply in this case, and that is why *preference* does not require a double *r*.

(10) A word ending with *ll* omits one *l* when a suffix beginning with a consonant is added to the word. For example:
Skill becomes *skilful*.
Full becomes *fulsome*.
Exceptions are *illness, smallness, stillness*.

(11) The letters *ei* follow *c*, but *ie* follow any other letter. Thus we write *receive*, but *believe*.

There are exceptions to this rule, but in almost every case the word itself gives a sufficient clue to the spelling. For instance, take *neighbour*. According to the rule, it should be *nieghbour*, but the sound tells us at once that this is out of the question.

The plural of nouns

(1) The general rule for forming the plural of a noun is to add an *s* to the singular. For example:
Cat becomes *cats*.

(2) Nouns ending in *s, ss, sh*, a soft *ch, x* or *z*, form their plural by adding *es* to the singular. For example:
Gas becomes *gases*.
Lass becomes *lasses*.
Thrush becomes *thrushes*.
Church becomes *churches*.
Box becomes *boxes*.
Chintz becomes *chintzes*.

The above rule only applies to the ending *ch* when it is soft, as in *church*. If the *ch* is hard, as in *monarch*, rule 1 applies and an *s* is added. For example:

Monarch becomes *monarchs*.

(3) Nouns ending in *f* or *fe* form their plurals by changing the *fo* or *fe* into *ves*. For example:

Loaf becomes *loaves*.

Life becomes *lives*.

However, there are many exceptions to this rule, and the following should be remembered:

Chief becomes *chiefs*.

Dwarf becomes *dwarfs*.

Fife becomes *fifes*.

Grief becomes *griefs*.

Gulf becomes *gulfs*.

Hoof can be either *hoofs* or *hooves*.

Proof becomes *proofs*.

Reef becomes *reefs*.

Scarf can be either *scarfs* or *scarves*.

Strife becomes *strifes*.

(4) Nouns ending in *y*, preceded by a consonant, change the *y* into *i* and add *es*. For example:

Lady becomes *ladies*.

If the *y* is preceded by a vowel, Rule 1 applies and an *s* is merely added. For example:

Boy becomes *boys*.

(5) Nouns ending in *o*, preceded by a consonant, form their plurals by adding *es*. For example:

Potato becomes *potatoes*.

Hero becomes *heroes*.

Negro becomes *negroes*.

But there are exceptions such as the following:

Octavo becomes *octavos*.

Piano becomes *pianos*.

Portico becomes *porticos.*
Proviso becomes *provisos.*
Tyro becomes *tyros.*
If the final *o* is preceded by a vowel, the plural is formed in the ordinary way, be adding *s*. Thus
Folio becomes *folios.*

(6) Some nouns have exceptional plurals, as *ox* becomes *oxen*, *mouse* becomes *mice*, and *child* becomes *children.*

(7) Compound nouns form their plurals by making the chief word into the plural. For example:
Mouse-trap becomes *mouse-traps.*
Mother-in-law becomes *mothers-in-law.*

It will be clear from all the above that English grammar is full of inconsistencies and that almost every rule has many exceptions. If you are in any doubt, consult a dictionary or reference book.

INDEX